SPORTS INJURIES

A
Unique Guide
to Self-diagnosis
and
Rehabilitation

SPORTS INJURIES

Dr Malcolm Read
with Paul Wade

BRESLICH & FOSS

LONDON

*To my wife Rosemary and
our children Jeremy and
Stephanie*

Breslich & Foss
43 Museum Street
London WC1A 1LY

Text © Malcolm Read and Paul Wade 1984
Illustrations © Breslich & Foss 1984

Page layout: Roger Daniels
Cover design: Chameleon
Illustrations: Don Parry
Additional research by Katherine Arnold

This book was produced with the help of Le Coq Sportif
and Scholl Sports Aid Division

British Library Cataloguing in Publication Data
Read, Malcolm
    Sports injuries.
    1. Sports—Accidents and injuries
    I. Title   II. Wade, Paul
    617′.1027   RD97
ISBN 1 85004 015 X Hbk
ISBN 1 85004 011 7 Pbk

Photoset in Great Britain by
Fakenham Photosetting Ltd, Fakenham, Norfolk
and printed by
Cambus Litho, East Kilbride, Scotland

First published in 1984
Reprinted 1984

Contents

How to get the most out of this book   6

1 HOW TO AVOID INJURIES IN THE FIRST PLACE   7
Stretching exercises   9
Some sensible tips   15
ICE (Ice, Compression, Elevation)   24
Your sports injury kit   26

2 GUIDE TO TREATMENTS   27
A–Z of self and medical treatments   28
A–Z of common ailments and how to deal with them   31

3 TOP-TO-TOE GUIDE TO INJURIES: DIAGNOSIS, CAUSE, TREATMENT AND TRAINING   34
How to use this section   36
Head   39
Neck and shoulder   42
Neck and chest   44
Shoulder   46
Elbow   51
Wrist and hand   56
Back   60
Living and training with back problems   64
Hip and pelvis   67
Upper leg   72
Knee   76
Lower leg   85
Ankle   90
Foot and toes   94

4 HOW TO RECOVER FROM AN INJURY: MALCOLM READ'S TRAINING LADDERS FOR REHABILITATION   99

5 SPORT-BY-SPORT GUIDE TO TECHNICAL INJURIES   128

6 A–Z OF MEDICAL TERMS   155

How to get the most out of this book

Topclass sportsmen and women have to be superbly fit and properly prepared, yet even they suffer sports injuries. Some are serious enough to require medical attention and specialist treatment; others are relatively minor and respond to simple home care. What many athletes do not realize, however, is that some injuries can be the result of poor technique rather than stress and strain. This applies to participants at all levels, from the weekend enthusiast to the international competitor.

Dr Malcolm Read, a former Olympic competitor and now a medical adviser to the British Olympic Association, has seen sports medicine make great advances in the last decade, and his knowledge and experience are packed into this book.

Since most injuries can be prevented, he starts by advising you how to prepare properly. Stretching exercises for warming up and down are recommended and some sensible though simple precautions listed. A sports injury kit is a major essential and should always be nearby when sportsmen and women are either training or practising their sport. Some injuries are obviously serious, but you can still be of help until the arrival of a qualified person. Similarly, there are a host of bumps and bruises so common that everyone knows how to treat them—or do they? Would you bandage a blister or prick it? Read chapter 2. Then there are the less obvious injuries—ones that hurt when you pick up a racquet or run up a hill. Locate the pain in chapter 3, its causes and cure.

In chapter 4, Dr Read's unique training ladders show you how to regain your general fitness; and in chapter 5 you can find out which common technical faults cause injuries in your particular sport and how to prevent, treat or alleviate these.

Sports medicine is still a relatively new field, so specialist sports doctors are few and far between. This book will help you understand your injuries, get back into action afterwards and, perhaps most important, prevent problems recurring.

HOW TO
AVOID INJURIES IN THE
FIRST PLACE

Three simple rules

Eighty per cent of all sports injuries could be avoided if only sportsmen and women at all levels prepared properly for training and competition.

1 Be fit for your individual sport!

Even if you are generally 'fit', you need to be fit enough for the rigours of your particular sport. Methodical exercise (not violent, sudden efforts) should be used to build up the correct balance of flexibility, strength and endurance. A good coaching book will set out the exercises required.

2 Warm up and warm down thoroughly!

Even if your body is not highly tuned and superfit, it will perform better when warm—like a car engine. Warming up is more than spending just a few seconds flapping the arms, as the stretching exercises on p 9 show. Set aside 15 minutes for these and at least another five minutes to warm down. This will prevent stiff, sore muscles the next day and also, when correctly executed, increase your general fitness.

3 Use the right equipment and technique!

Your body is different in shape and size from anyone else's, so the design of a running shoe or the weight of a racquet head, the position of a rowing seat or ski binding must suit you individually. Technique is just as important. If faulty, it could cause an injury—whether paddling a kayak or putting the shot. Again, training a certain way may suit one person's body build and produce a gold medal, but if those methods produce injuries in you, use other techniques that don't!

Finally, if there is one lesson to be learnt, it is that millions of injuries are caused not in matches but in training. 'Overuse' occurs when one part of the body has been asked to do too much, and **quality** rather than **quantity** of work is what counts. More is not necessarily better! Similarly, if you have been totally inactive for years, you should allow about one month's proper training for every year of inactivity to regain your past level of fitness.

Stretching exercises

These exercises can be done at any time of the day or night as part of an effort to keep fit as well as for warming up before training and competition. In addition to stretching muscles, tendons and ligaments, there is evidence that proper stretching actually builds strength.

Always *press* through the tension in each exercise. Never *bounce*. When you reach the point where it begins to hurt, hold it there for 10–20 sec, then relax. Gradually you will get more and more limber. It helps to breathe out gently as you stretch.

Throughout the book, certain exercises will be recommended by number as being particularly beneficial in aiding recovery.

1 Stretches calf muscles, reducing risk of Achilles tear. Forearms flat on wall, toes and feet together pointing straight forward. Slowly press hips forward keeping knees straight. Hold when you feel 'pull' in calves.

2 Calf muscle stretch where no wall available, also reduces risk of Achilles problem.
Feet comfortably apart, keep trunk upright with weight over rear leg. Rear foot *must* point straight forward. Move front foot slowly forward. Hold when stretch felt in calf of rear leg. Repeat with opposite foot forward.

3 Stretches shoulder and upper back muscles. Useful for swimmers, racquet sports players, etc.
Clasp hands behind and slightly above head height. Press shoulders and elbows backwards. Hold when 'pull' felt.

4 Stretches muscle on inside of groin, vital for quick side-to-side movements, fast acceleration.
Stand with feet wide apart, hands on hips, trunk upright. Bending right leg, put weight over straight left leg. Do not lean forward. Hold when 'pull' felt in groin of straight leg. Increase stretch by leaning further over straight leg. Keep bottom in. Repeat to other side.

5 Stretches upper back and hamstring muscles at back of thigh.
Support yourself with hands on hips, legs together. Keep back and legs as straight as possible. In time, straight legs will touch ground. Hold when 'pull' felt in back and legs.

7 Another exercise for hip and back mobility.
Stand comfortably, with hands clasped in front of you. Slowly rotate as far as you can go to right. Hold. Repeat to left.

6 Helps side-to-side mobility.
Stand comfortably, clasp hands at full stretch above head. Keeping trunk upright, lean sideways. Don't lean forward! Hold when 'pull' felt down side. Repeat to other side.

8 Stretches important quadriceps muscles on front of thigh.
Stand on right leg, hold left foot in left hand and pull knee backwards. Keep back straight. Hold when 'pull' felt on front of thigh. Repeat on other side.

9 This stretches injury-prone hamstring muscle at back of thigh.
Stand upright with feet wide apart, hands on hips. Push bottom backwards, then pivot forward from hips, with back straight and chest thrusting forwards. Only then drop hands well in front of feet. Hold when 'pull' felt at back of knees. As flexibility increases, move feet closer together.

10 Hamstrings, quads and adductors benefit from this 'hurdler's stretch'.
Try to get legs at right angles. Then keeping back straight, try to place chest over straight leg. Hold when 'pull' felt at back of knee. Alternate legs. If very stiff, grasp back of calf and pull forward. Also, lean backwards (in line with straight leg) to stretch muscles on bent leg. Do not lean away from bent leg.

11 Stretches calf, quads and hips.
With hands on hips, move into lunge position, both feet pointing forwards. Keep trunk upright. Drop weight towards bent front leg. Hold when 'pull' felt on front of rear leg thigh. Repeat with opposite leg.

12 Stretches upper end of hamstring.
Put right heel up on wall, chair, etc., preferably hip high. Keep back straight and try to put chest on knee. Hold when 'pull' felt in buttock and behind knee. Alternate legs.

Some sensible tips

As we have said, as many as 80 per cent of all injuries could be avoided. The following A–Z of sensible tips tells you how to forestall potential hazards and help your performance. Read through it, and you will find more ways of preparing yourself properly for the fun and competition of sport and leisure.

Did you know you should never train if you have flu? Or that pregnancy is no excuse for stopping exercise? Or that gumshields (mouthpieces) are now light, cheap and easy to wear? Read on—and think before you play.

Aches and pains   Indications that something is wrong. Enduring pain can increase degree of injury. Pinpoint problem and treat it properly.

Aeroplanes   Low cabin pressure causes swollen feet and gassy fluids distend stomach, so wear loose, comfortable clothes for long journeys. Drink plenty of water as air-conditioning causes dehydration.

Age   No handicap, but take sensible precautions before engaging in a sport. With age, body's natural elasticity disappears and healing slows. With less time for exercise, better to do 10–15 min daily than go all out once a week. Get fit to play, don't play to get fit. Readjust expectations, using skill and experience to replace speed and fitness. See: Senior citizens.

Alcohol   Not harmful in moderation. A little may calm nervous tremor but it also decreases hand–eye coordination. Its effect is to dilate the blood vessels on the body's surface, giving a false sense of warmth while actually cooling the body faster. Therefore, a drink before going out in very cold weather can be dangerous.

Altitude   Skiers, climbers and backpackers may feel tired and breathless, with hammering headache. Allow time to acclimatize (days or weeks depending on height) to less oxygen in air. Drink more water, as sun reflected off snow and wearing heavy clothes are dehydrating.

Altitude sickness   Difficulty in breathing due to waterlogging of lungs. Move immediately at least 610 m (2,000 ft) lower.

Asthma

Asthmatics suffer because they cannot get enough air to their lungs. However, many worldclass sportsmen and women are asthmatics. The answer can be to train in a series of short sessions with a rest in between. Swimming is beneficial, as the damp air in indoor pools is free of irritating pollens, etc. Exercise might induce 'wheeziness' in some people: this may be helped by using Salbutamol (Ventolin) and sodium cromoglycate. See doctor. Cold weather can also spark this off, so use above drugs and put mask or scarf across nose and mouth to warm inhaled air.

Back

Aches and pains can be avoided. Exercise may be taken despite pain in back. See pp 64–6.

Bone growth

Stops mid to late teens. Damage, from overuse, weight training, etc., may stunt or alter growth of injured part.

Bow legs/Bandy legs

May be more prone to injury, particularly in repetitive movements of long-distance running.

Breasts

Bouncing, unsupported breasts may be painful after exercise due to friction or torn tissue. Sports bras are widely available and support without restricting movement. Blows to breast do *not* cause cancer. Damaged breast fat, however, is very tender, may feel like lump and takes time to heal. Check with doctor. See: Neck and chest, p 44.

Bunny hops

Should be banned from training regimes. Too many cartilages are torn and very few sports require leg strength in full squat position. So what are you training?

Check-ups

Check present, not future health. Useful for older men and women, to ascertain any problems in taking up sport.

Chewing gum

Inhaled chewing gum can kill. Although gum is often used by top sports stars, it should *not* be used during intense physical activity or when sudden 'avoiding' movements may occur.

Children

Must not be sacrificed to feed ego of coach and parent. No champion junior should become a wrecked senior. Build up stresses gradually and ensure correct techniques. Do not use age to match children (especially in contact sports)—think about matching for size.

Clothing

Use clothing appropriate to movements of chosen sport, not necessarily expensive but comfortable. Jeans, for example, are restrictive for jogging, while nylon socks do not absorb sweat. Light or reflective clothing should be worn by runners and joggers at night.

Coffee

Useful before endurance events like marathon as stimulates body to release fats into bloodstream. Muscles can therefore work longer before drawing on reserve glycogen (muscle energy source). Caffeine makes some feel more alert.

Cold weather

Dress properly, protecting toes, nose, fingers, ears · especially. Use lightweight waterproof suit over training clothes to reduce wind-chill effect. May affect some sufferers from asthma (allergic or exercise induced). Use sodium cromoglycate (Intal) or asthma inhaler (Salbutamol, Ventolin) 15 min before exercise. Warm up air by breathing through mask or scarf.

Colds

See: Head colds, Flu.

Dehydration

Often causes bad sporting performance, even in temperate climates. Increased activity means increased sweating, requiring greater fluid intake, especially when temperature is over 27°C (80°F). Distance event competitors (running, cycling, canoeing, etc.) should take care. Check urine colour: if clear, no dehydration; if yellow, drink more water; not passing urine, drink more water. See: Salt.

Diabetics

Can take part in almost all sports after discussion and planning with doctor.

Diarrhoea, traveller's

Infection of the intestine. In tropical countries:
1 Always wash hands before meals
2 Peel all fruit including grapes
3 Only drink water that is safe—in approved hotel; otherwise boil or use sterilizing tablets
4 Do not eat ice-creams or swallow ice cubes from outside approved hotel
5 Beware salads—cooked food is safer
6 Get appropriate inoculations, e.g. cholera, typhoid
7 Consult doctor re medicines.

Diet

A normal, balanced diet is essential during training. *Marathon runner's diet* (carbohydrate load, pasta party) for more energy and less dehydration: Load muscles with extra glycogen (muscle energy source) by training hard over 3–4 days on normal or high protein, low carbohydrate diet, then training lightly for 3 days before race on high carbohydrate, low protein diet.
Prematch diet: Eat 3 hours before match if possible but at least 1½–2 hours before. High energy, quickly digested foods such as pasta, cakes and desserts are best. Low energy, slowly digested foods like steak only in small amounts if at all. Breakfast before morning matches should

be 'continental' rather than English or American.
Tournament diet: Matches over several days deplete
glycogen in muscles. Replace by going on high
carbohydrate diet.

Dieting

Cutting down on calories is main way to lose weight.
Exercise tones body rather than taking off weight. Eat
sensible, well-balanced diet and exercise regularly.

Dirty clothes

Clean clothes *are* important. Old sweat contains germs
which can cause irritating skin problems.

Drugs

Certain ones are banned and some competitions test for
traces of these in urine. Asthmatics and hay fever sufferers
must check months before important competitions to see if
alteration in drugs required. Even patent cough
medicines, vitamins, etc., must be checked with team
doctors in case they are 'drug positive'.

Eating

See: Diet.

Epileptics

Like diabetics, can take part in most sports. Exceptions
are events where blows to head are likely or underwater
sports or climbing, where a fit could be fatal.

Equipment

Choose equipment that suits you and feels comfortable to
use. Need not be most expensive, but beware of
'hand-me-downs'. See: Clothing.

Exposure

See: Hypothermia.

Eyes

Vulnerable in many sports. If protection advisable, wear
it—using protective goggles in badminton, squash, even
tennis is not 'soft' but sensible. Swimmers often use
goggles. Skiers and sailors need to guard against dazzling
reflected light with polaroid-type glasses.

Fatigue

Another warning, usually from muscles running out of
energy and becoming choked on waste products.

Field of play

Check area of play (beach, court, pool, etc.) for possible
hazards, e.g. broken bottle, discarded can, ice, oil, etc.
Essential in mat areas for gymnastics or martial arts, etc.,
where even projecting radiators can be dangerous.

Fitness

Are you fit to play? Hurling yourself into action after a layoff
is asking for trouble (anything from stiff, aching muscles to
serious strains and sprains). Each sport requires *specific*
fitness—check coaching manuals. Only by exercising
enthusiastically at least 30 min every 2 days can you be
'fit'. But remember to build up gradually: 10–15 min daily

is better than going flat out for an hour once a week!

Flat feet
Flattening of arch between heelbone and toes which causes strains when overused. Arch support, exercises, orthotics may help.

Flexibility, lack of
Results in pulled muscles. Warm-up stretching essential as short muscles particularly, with no reserve in length or elasticity, may tear because of sudden slip or bend. Stretching may also contribute to muscle power.

Flu
More serious than a cold. *Never train with a temperature or with aching muscles due to fever.* See: Head colds.

Genitals
Need protection in contact sports or when hard ball is used. Men should wear jockstrap at all times and hard cup (box) even for practising games where abdominal blows are common.

Gumshields/Mouthpieces
No longer big and uncomfortable. Nowadays lightweight, translucent and cheap. Should be custom-made for proper fit as may be dangerous otherwise. Not only protect teeth, but also help reduce likelihood of concussion in contact sports.

Hair
Keep out of eyes with headband: Floppy hair could blind at a crucial moment.

Hay fever
Allergy to pollens, especially grass. Antihistamines and decongestants have disadvantage of causing drowsiness. Some drugs may be banned in competitions, so check with doctor *before* season begins. Special drugs and desensitizing injections that are not banned are now available.

Head colds
Caused by virus. Antibiotics no help so take aspirin or other painkiller, rest, plenty of fluids, nose drops (4 days maximum), throat lozenges (3 days maximum) and menthol inhalation. See: Flu.

Heat/Hot weather
Wear proper lightweight, airy clothing (cotton or cotton/mixture) and cover head and nape of neck. A single glass of water may quench your thirst but body may still be short of water. It takes 2–3 days to adjust and tell you more fluid is needed to replace water lost by increased sweating. See: Dehydration, Sunburn.

High arches
Can cause injury since foot does not hit ground properly. However, most problems are on top of foot, where shoe may not be cut high enough so laces are too tight.

Hypothermia

Dangerous chilling of body. Often occurs in water-related sports like canoeing. Described as 'number one killer of outdoor recreationists' by US Forest Service, who say it is 'rapid, progressive mental and physical collapse accompanying the chilling of the inner core of the human body ... caused by exposure to cold, aggravated by wet, wind and exhaustion'. Waterproof outer layer of clothing helps retain body heat. For hill-walking, waterproof trousers as well as anoraks are advised, as wet legs can lose large amounts of heat—protecting upper body is not enough. Get anyone who has fallen in water out as soon as possible. If help available, remain still in water to conserve heat, as swimming warms limbs but cools core temperature. Hypothermia victims are irrational, with slow responses, speech and vision difficulties and cold to touch. Pulse and breathing are weak. Recovery: remove wet clothes and warm gradually in (a) sleeping bag, (b) between two bodies. Hill-walkers and mountaineers should carry large plastic bags for this eventuality as wet and wind chill fastest of all. Application of sudden intense heat is dangerous. Seek medical help urgently.

Indigestion

Pain in pit of stomach, often due to tension. Antacids give relief. Some sports, like cycling, encourage heartburn and stomach gas to press under diaphragm. Use antacids and peppermint to bring up wind before competition and avoid gassy drinks. One teaspoon of bicarbonate of soda (cooking soda) in an eggcup of water is a simple antacid.

Influenza

See: Flu.

Jet lag

Your body needs 24 hours per hour of time change to fully adjust. Therefore fatigue may be felt when exercising normally during first few days of adjustment.

Jewellery

Should never be worn for sporting activity, especially pendant necklaces, earrings, finger rings or watches, as can cause injury to wearer or opponent.

Kit, sports injury

See p 26. Even the occasional sportsman or woman should have an injury kit bag handy.

Knock knees

Can put extra strain on knees. Corrective orthotics in shoe may help; consult orthopedist.

Legs, unequal length

Non-sports doctors feel this has little effect unless difference is at least 2 cm (1 in). However, runners may suffer from leg strain and back pain. Raising heel, or using extra inner sole, will help shorter leg. Similarly, reduction in heel height of shoe on good leg could help.

Liniment

Smells sporty, but its warm sensation has no deep-down effect on muscle and is no substitute for proper warm-up stretching.

Menstruation

See: Periods.

Mouth

See: Gumshields/Mouthpieces.

Muscle imbalance

To move a joint, one muscle shortens as its opposite lengthens. If one is stronger, strains occur. Sometimes result of enthusiastic but poorly scheduled weight-training. See coach.

Nails, finger and toe

Should be trimmed frequently.
Toenails should be cut square to avoid ingrowing.
Fingernails should be short and neat, especially for catching sports.

Overtraining/Overuse

Most common cause of injury in non-contact sports. Do not work through pain—rather build up body to withstand workload. Training schedules must be individual, to suit specific body.

Overweight

Athletic activity can help reduce weight if in conjunction with specific diet and training plan. A heavy build puts more strain on lower leg so be careful when choosing footwear. If taking up sport after years of inactivity, have medical check-up and ease gently into action.

Periods

Do not necessarily diminish athletic performance. World and Olympic titles have been won at all stages of monthly cycle. Painful periods with premenstrual fluid retention can be eased. Consult doctor. See: Pill, the.

Physically handicapped

The Stoke Mandeville Games for the physically handicapped were initiated by Sir Ludwig Guttman in 1952. His theory that sport can help regenerate muscle and provide mental stimulus to give even the seriously handicapped the will to survive has now gained international acceptance. Similar games for the handicapped, the Special Olympics, take place annually in the United States.

Pigeon toes

Feet that turn inwards so toes on one foot point at toes on other. Most problems occur from overuse, as in long-distance running.

Pill, the

May be useful to control painful periods. On medical advice, period may be postponed by carrying on with following month's supply (or even for few extra days) without normal seven-day break. Then continue as normal.

This could be done preferably 2–3 months before important event.

Pregnancy

If active before pregnancy, women can continue sport as long as is comfortable with no ill-effects. Baby is well protected in bag of fluid. However, stop exercise if spotting of blood or low stomach or back pain. Consult doctor.

Pulse rate

Fit person will do same amount of exercise at slower heart rate than less fit, who will draw on more reserves for extra work. Stamina, or aerobic, training makes heart stronger and lungs more efficient. Normal heart cannot be damaged by exercise.

Salt

Lost from body in sweat and must be replaced by adding it to food and drinks or even by taking salt tablets. But drinking enough water is most important. See: Dehydration. Special drinks containing salt and other chemicals lost in sweat also have sugar for energy.

Senior citizens

Exercise doesn't prevent ageing, but puts off its advances by giving sense of 'feeling good', reducing tiredness and listlessness and strengthening heart. Consult doctor on which sport and how much activity, especially if beginning after 50.

Sex

By all accounts, better when both partners are fit and healthy. Even at professional level, sportsmen and women feel no need to abstain before competition. If anything, relaxation after lovemaking calms prematch tensions.

Smoking

Is bad for you. A drop of nicotine on an artery contracts it, allowing less blood through. This causes high blood pressure and means less blood gets to muscles. Smoke clogs fine filters of lungs and various chemicals displace oxygen in red blood cells.

Socks

Should be kept up by broad tape (not string, which could cut off circulation). Holes can cause blisters. See: Clothing.

Sun/Sunburn

Back of neck, nose, shoulders, tops of feet and knees especially vulnerable. Build up exposure slowly. Filter creams may be particularly effective but research has indicated some cause other problems so discuss with doctor. Water and snow may double sun's effect by reflection and swimming cools down body's warning sense of discomfort or heat—use moisturizing creams after exposure. Prevention is better than cure, but for serious sunburn see doctor.

Surfaces

Hard surfaces jar feet, ankles and legs, so choose footwear carefully for marathon running, real tennis, etc. Soft, muddy fields and artificial grass also pose problems.

Sweatbands

Help keep sweat and long hair out of eyes, but should not be so tight as to restrict blood supply to scalp. (Sometimes smear of petroleum jelly over eyebrows helps sweat run away from eyes.) Armbands prevent sweat running onto grip (for racquet games).

Taping

Joints

May strengthen injured part, particularly ligaments surrounding joint. Stops relevant bones from stretching too far apart. Once ligament painfree, continue taping or elastic support further 6 weeks so full strength is regained. Then (there are two schools of thought), either: (a) always strap joint for activity, thus preventing damage and keeping joint 'stable' but spreading 'torque' or load onto other joints; or (b) stop strapping, so that 'torque' may be shared by this joint as well as others. This last theory says that the 'immobile' ('stable') joint can't take its share of load and so overloads others.

Muscles

Taping may act like outer skeleton, supporting muscle so load is spread away from damaged area.

Self-taping

Consult physiotherapist and experienced adviser if possible. Shave hair or apply tincture of benzoin compound or thin rubber underwrap to stop strapping burns.

Teeth

See: Gumshields/Mouthpieces. Regular dental checks will prevent sudden abscess ruining competition or recreation.

Temperature, raised

Stop all training. No *sporting* injury (apart from dehydration) makes your temperature rise. Resume training only when feeling completely well again.

Tetanus

Sportsmen and women should have regular protective injections. See doctor.

Varicose veins

Exercise generally improves veins but increased blood flow may be painful. Elastic supports should be worn.

ICE

ICE is the simplest and most efficient remedy for a host of injuries, and yet many sportsmen and women disregard this valuable aid. **DO NOT IGNORE THIS ADVICE.** The combination of **I** (Ice), **C** (Compression) and **E** (Elevation) helps to reduce swelling and restrict spread of bruising, both of which can slow down the healing process. As soon as possible after sustaining injury you should apply ice and bandaging and raise the injured part. At the same time you can enjoy a drink after your match, happy in the knowledge that you are doing something positive to heal your injury. **The first 6 hours are the most vital.**

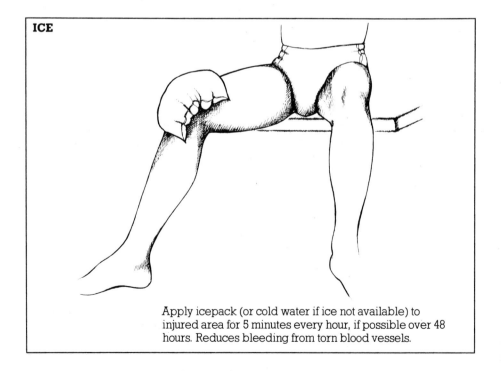

ICE

Apply icepack (or cold water if ice not available) to injured area for 5 minutes every hour, if possible over 48 hours. Reduces bleeding from torn blood vessels.

COMPRESSION

Bandage injured area firmly (but not so tightly that it is uncomfortable) in order to contain swelling.

ELEVATION

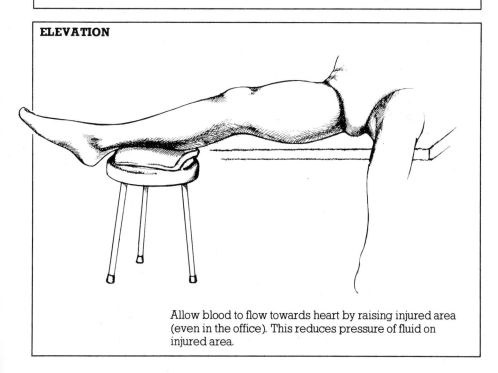

Allow blood to flow towards heart by raising injured area (even in the office). This reduces pressure of fluid on injured area.

Your sports injury kit

There is one essential standby for the sportsman or woman—the sports injury kit. Think ahead: don't ruin your day for lack of something as simple as a plaster (adhesive bandage). There are made-up first-aid kits on the market, but it's just as easy (and cheaper!) to assemble your own.

Stage 1 is our recommended minimum, but the more you participate and the better you are at a sport the more you need to be prepared. Add stage 2, then 3—and even 4 for team events.

STAGE 1

Box of different sized dressing plasters (adhesive bandages)
10×10 cm (4×4 in approx.) sterile gauze pads (clean, ironed handkerchief will do)
5 cm (2 in) gauze bandages
2·5 cm (1 in) elastic bandages
7·5 cm (3 in) elastic bandages
Icepack. Plastic bags for ice (or packets of frozen peas—ideal shape for applying to injuries)
Scissors, for medical use
Sports Injuries and first-aid book

STAGE 2

Safety pins
Nail clippers
Scissors with 5 cm (2 in) blades, for general use
Needle
Cotton wool (cotton balls)
Antiseptic fluid
Tweezers
Rubber bands
Petroleum jelly
Silicone cream
Baby oil or oil of wintergreen (contained in most massage creams) for massage
Orthopaedic felt for padding
Elastic knee/ankle/elbow support
Sling
Aspirin or non-aspirin painkiller
Antacid tablets
Foot powder

STAGE 3

Strapping tape
Elastic strapping tape
Underwrap
Tincture of benzoin compound to stop tape hurting skin
Portable razor
Steristrip or adhesive plaster sutures
Aerosol coolant spray
Plastic or 'second skin' product for blisters
Eyebath and eyewash
Fluid replacement drink

STAGE 4

Fracture boards or blow-up splints
Stretcher

Warning Too often friends will borrow the scissors or use the last plaster (adhesive bandage) without replacing it, so stick a list of contents on the outside of your bag and check regularly. Make sure the telephone number of your doctor or sports injury expert is written or taped on it.

GUIDE
TO
TREATMENTS

A–Z of self and medical treatments

The A–Z of treatments—both self and medically prescribed—tells you what some of the more commonly used forms of treatment for sports injuries actually do to help you. It is followed by a list of common ailments or minor injuries and advice on how to cope with these.

Antibiotics Chemicals that kill off bacteria which cause infections. Do not work against viruses such as flu or common cold.

Anti-bruise cream Contains anti-inflammatory drug to reduce inflammation.

Anti-inflammatory drugs Neutralize inflammation produced by damage to body. Known as non-steroidal anti-inflammatory drugs (NSAIDS). Aspirin is best known; butazolidin has long been used on horses, and there are many others on the market. Must be taken with food as indigestion and even stomach ulcers can be caused. Should be prescribed by doctor.

Aspirin Excellent anti-inflammatory agent—accelerates healing. Take 2 tablets with each meal at minimum 4-hr intervals; also before going to bed with, say, glass of milk. Continue for 48 hr.

Braced knee support External metal hinged support, makes it possible to play non-contact sport when cruciate knee ligaments are damaged.

Compress Firm bandaging that may hold hot/cold, etc., pad onto damaged area.

Cortisone injection Reduces inflammation. Very useful drug, but overuse may lead to problems. May be *more* painful for 48 hr after injection.

Draining with needle Releasing fluid from injured area.

Effluage Massage technique that works damaged cells and fluid away from injury towards heart.

Enzyme cream Contains chemical to increase blood supply and 'digest' bruise.

Epidural injection

Spinal injection (used commonly for women giving birth) that numbs and paralyses lower limbs and pelvic area. May be given in dilute form to avoid temporary paralysis of lower legs and will then not start to take effect before 4–5 days. Helps to stop sciatic pain.

Faradism, differential

Selective machine making one muscle contract just ahead of another, so altering muscle balance.

Heel raise

Rubber insertion in shoes to alter angle of foot as it strikes ground in walking or running.

Ice

Cold water; cooling gel; chemical freezer; anything that cools painful area.

ICE

Ice, Compression, Elevation—the most underrated way of dealing with injuries (sometimes referred to as RICE, to include Rest). (See p 24.)

Injections

In this book, refers to those that have to be made directly at seat of injury.

Ladders

Malcolm Read's rehabilitation plans. See chapter 4.

Manipulation, self, surgical

Technique of locking some joints so that others may be freed.

Massage

Designed to warm up muscles and skin and to help clear fluid and bruising, depending on technique used.
Cross-frictional: Rubs skin *across* muscle and tendons rather than *along* their length.
Deep friction: Uses firm pressure to get at deeper tissues.

Menthol crystals, inhalation of

Clears sinus and nasal passages. Only requires about two crystals dissolved in hot water. Cheap and easy to obtain and not 'drug positive'.

Mobilization

Moving joint or muscle through its normal range.

Muscle relaxant

Drug that reduces tension or excitability of a muscle. May be mild or major, as used in surgery.

Nose drops

Reduce swelling in nasal passages, improving airflow. If used more than four days, however, may perpetuate nasal problem.

Orthotics

Various devices made to fit in shoe, aimed at correcting or altering foot position to help overuse strains of foot, ankle, knee or back. Range from heel and arch inserts to expensive, custom-made insoles. Useful, but *not* cure-all.

Painkillers

May work to stop brain from telling you it hurts or may calm painful area, e.g. aspirin.

Physiotherapy

Includes massage, heating and mobilization treatments.

Plaster cast

Plaster of Paris cast that prevents movement of joints or broken bones.

Sling

Triangular bandage tied around neck to support weight of forearm and elbow. *Collar and cuff:* Supports injury from wrist to neck.

Splint

Solid object to which damaged part may be strapped. Prevents painful movement of joint or fracture.

Strapping

Used to support muscle or joint, giving added strength. May be stretch elastic or non-stretch adhesive tape. (See diagram, p 89.)

Sugar injection

Contains dextrose sugar; used to promote growth and strength of back ligaments.

Support corset

Strap-on corset that may have strengthening bones (plastic or metal). Used to strengthen back. Reminder of correct back position when gardening, lifting, etc.

Sutures

Stitches of catgut, nylon or silk. Steristrip, butterfly plaster: adhesive stitches for cut skin.

Traction

Pulling apart from either end to allow damaged parts (broken bones, spinal disc) to return to normal position.

Ultrasound

High-frequency soundwave that vibrates and loosens scar tissue, also produces heat at deeper level; can be used to examine muscles.

Warm baths

Increase blood flow and warm joints. Damaged joints may then be moved more easily.

'Water' tablets

Make you pass more urine. Often taken by people with damaged hearts so that amount of fluid to be pumped around is less; may ease premenstrual breast engorgement. Danger of rapid dehydration, however, if used to 'make the weight'.

Wobble board

Balancing board designed to improve ankle, knee and hip coordination.

A–Z of common ailments and how to deal with them

There are many common or minor injuries or discomforts that can occur in almost any part of the body—if you fall off a bike or wear tight new running shoes for example. Look here for those common ailments and advice on how to avoid and treat them.

Abrasion	See: Graze.
Athlete's foot	Fungus growing between toes picked up in swimming-pools and communal showers. Avoid by wearing 'flip flops'/thonged sandals and drying feet thoroughly; powdering gives extra protection. Treat with antifungal powder, liquid or cream and consult doctor if persistent.
Blister	Caused by persistent rubbing against unprotected skin before it can form protective callous. Avoid by slowly building up, and varying, training and by protecting pressure areas (using gloves, plasters/adhesive bandages or special protectors). To treat blister: (a) clean with antiseptic; (b) use pin sterilized in flame until red hot then cooled to prick 'bubble', releasing fluid; (c) leave skin in place, cover with gauze pad, then adhesive tape. If spreading red discoloration of skin around blister (or callous), seek medical advice for possible infection. For activity, use slippery plaster and grease outside of tape with soap. Two pairs of socks may prevent recurrence on soles of feet.
Bruise	Blood escaping through damaged area and trapped under skin. Use ICE to restrict swelling. Bruise may travel and appear away from injury (always nearer feet, due to gravity).
Bunion	Bone spur on inside (ball) of foot, when big toe points in at angle to other toes. Soft sponge pad between it and second toe helps straighten big toe. Arch support with pad under big toe and orthotics may correct flattening of arch due to 'treading over' on inside of foot. If inflamed and painful, use aspirin (at mealtimes) and ICE after activity. Occasionally requires surgery.

Burn

Caused by sliding after fall on real or artificial turf, cycle track, etc. Treat as for Graze.

Callous

Protective thickening of skin layers where rubbing occurs. Forms over bases of fingers in all games where hand holds instrument (racquet games, hockey, etc.) but most spectacular in men's gymnastics. Should not be removed— just file off rough edges with pumice stone or emery paper.

Corn

Hard pad of skin over pressure area having small fluid sac below to allow hard pad to slide back and forward without damaging tissue underneath. If torn and infected, seek medical advice. Corn pads spread load away from pressure point. Claw toes and bunions should be treated and fit of shoes adjusted.

Cramp

Involuntary shortening of muscle. Exact cause unknown but poor coordination, poor blood supply, chilling (e.g. while swimming) or excessive salt loss (from extreme sweating) may have effect. Stretch muscle and massage firmly. Some drugs may help, so see doctor.

Cuts

Stop bleeding by pressing with clean cloth (ironed handkerchief is virtually sterile) or fingers. Elevate injured area if possible. Then use cold, running water to clean out dirt, grit, etc. Dab on antiseptic. If shallow, cover with gauze and adhesive tape; if deep, bring edges together with 'adhesive stitches' or see doctor.

Faintness

Warning all is not well. Sit with head between knees or lie down. Warm down after long run to avoid feeling faint again once you stand up.

Graze

When skin is scraped off from fall on rough or hard surface. Clean with running water, dry and apply antiseptic ointment if available; leave uncovered if possible (adhesive bandage keeps area moist, allowing bacteria to grow).

Groin itch/Jock rot/Jock itch/Dhobi itch, etc.

Infection caused by fungus. Ensure underclothes are clean; dry area well. Treat as Athlete's foot. Beware—some lotions sting when applied!

Scrape

See: Graze.

Stitch

Pain under ribs when running. Cause not known but may be effect of taking blood away from digestion and using it to provide oxygen for muscles. Another reason not to run too soon after eating.

Verruca wart

Wart on foot. Body weight drives wart inwards. Caused by virus, spread by contact, especially in showers and swimming pools. See doctor. Treat with chemicals or freezing gases, wear rubber swimsocks to prevent spreading to others. Use 'flip flops' or thongs in shower.

Winding

To counteract, breathe in 'short' then breathe out 'long' to relax muscles. Feeling should disappear after few minutes.

Warts

Virus infection on skin. Difficult to remove; treatments include stringent chemicals, freezing gases to burn out. Sometimes 'charmed' or hypnotized away!

3

TOP-TO-TOE
GUIDE TO INJURIES:
DIAGNOSIS,
CAUSE, TREATMENT
AND TRAINING

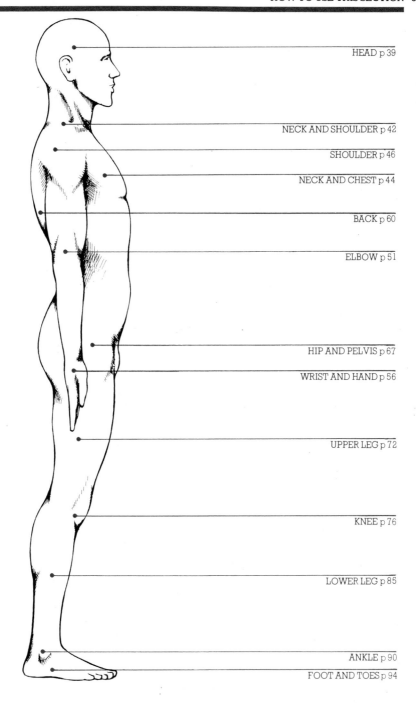

HEAD p 39

NECK AND SHOULDER p 42

SHOULDER p 46

NECK AND CHEST p 44

BACK p 60

ELBOW p 51

HIP AND PELVIS p 67

WRIST AND HAND p 56

UPPER LEG p 72

KNEE p 76

LOWER LEG p 85

ANKLE p 90

FOOT AND TOES p 94

How to use this section

Every effort has been made to cover all the most common sports injuries in this section. However, fractures have *not* been covered as they require immediate medical attention. If you cannot identify your injury, or if it does not respond to the treatment indicated, you are strongly advised to seek medical aid.

This section—the central part of the guide—tells you how to identify your sports injury, what has produced it, what you can do to help yourself and what are the likely medical treatments. Advice on training to get back to normal is also given. This is how to use it.

1

Turn to the part of the body that you have injured.
Head. Neck and shoulder. Neck and chest. Shoulder. Elbow. Wrist and hand. Back. Hip and pelvis. Upper leg. Knee. Lower leg. Ankle. Foot and toes.

If you do not find the area in the first part you try, look in one adjacent.

2

Now find the painful area or areas marked on the diagram that most nearly match your pain. Pain indicated on one side of the body also, of course, refers to pain on the opposite side.

3

You may find two or three names. The diagnostic tests which follow will help you to identify your injury, but you may have to try out all possibilities.

Diagnosis

An area round a joint may be painful because either the muscle and tendons or the joint and its ligaments have been damaged.

To test muscles and tendons, we must make the muscle work but not let the joint move. This is done by *trying* to make a particular movement and *blocking* it with your opposite hand or arm, the wall, furniture or a friend. This is called **resisted movement**.

To test a joint, we must stop the muscles working— harder to do—but still move the joint. Lift your arm (say) with your other hand or get a friend to do it. This is called **passive movement**.

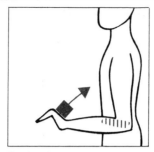 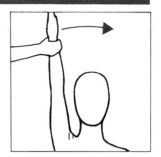

Resisted movement:
To test muscles and tendons
The arrow indicates the direction of attempted movement. The block under the arrow shows the point at which you must prevent this movement from taking place. The red area indicates where the pain will be felt.

Passive movement:
To test joints and ligaments
Move arm (say) as far as you can in the direction(s) indicated by the arrow. It may hurt early in the movement or only right at the end, and ligaments may require a little force applied at the end of the movement to show they are damaged. Do not try to show how much pain you can stand. If it hurts, it hurts. 'Hands' shown in diagrams indicate passive movement.

Note: In the few illustrations with neither block nor 'hands' you should make the movement yourself.

If these tests do not confirm your injury, move onto the next of your two or three names.

Cause

The physical origins of the injury will be given and may indicate that you should alter your technique and training in order to avoid it.

Treatment

Self: These are things you can do to help yourself.
Medical: Some of the treatments available from doctors.

Training

Some doctors will tell you what is wrong and then advise you just to rest or even let you return to matches before you have thoroughly recovered. However, no two injuries are ever exactly the same, so a recommended rest period is always somewhat arbitrary. The appropriate **ladder plan** for training (chapter 4) will show you how to rest the injured part but keep yourself as fit as possible. The ladders are designed to gradually load the injured part more and more without re-damaging it. The swimming, rowing, bike, patter, etc., routines referred to are also included in chapter 4, as well as the individual ladder plans.

Serious injuries warning

Serious injuries on the sports field require first-aid treatment. Medical help must be sought at once, so it is always sensible to have the telephone number of the nearest doctor, hospital or medical centre handy, however casual your level of competition. Some basic rules should be followed. In the case of a broken bone (fracture), strap the damaged part to a solid, unbendable object and move the victim as little as possible. Cover to keep warm but do not give anything to drink. If he or she has possible numbness in the limbs, this could mean a fractured spine. In this case, **do not move the victim at all.** This could only aggravate the injury. Wait for medical assistance. Cover to keep warm and give no liquids or painkillers. See also: Head, Neck and chest, Shoulder.

If a player loses consciousness because of a blow to the body, etc., place him or her as shown with clothing loosened. Remove gumshield (mouthpiece) or false teeth. To keep air passages clear, force chin upwards with fingers at angle of jaw.

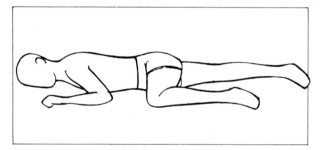

If a player stops breathing (or has taken in a lot of water in a water-sport accident), use artificial respiration techniques such as mouth-to-mouth or mouth-to-nose resuscitation.

Please note: This is not a first-aid manual, and it is a good idea to have some knowledge of first aid if you play any sport regularly.

Head

A strong, bony box containing the brain and various organs vital to the body's well-being. Injuries may be disfiguring or even disabling, yet too many sportsmen and women ignore the readily available protections like eye-goggles and gumshields. Only recently has the game of cricket, for example, accepted that a fast 'bouncer' or a well-struck shot hits the unprotected head like a missile.

Warning: Head and neck injuries can be very serious: (a) if there is numbness or 'pins and needles' sensation in arms and legs; or (b) if neither hand nor foot can be moved.
Do not move player—even if it means abandoning game! Get immediate medical help. NB Leak of clear fluid from nose or ears suggests fractured skull. Leak of blood from nose or ears should also be treated as fractured skull, but clear away blood to check if cut is cause of bleeding.

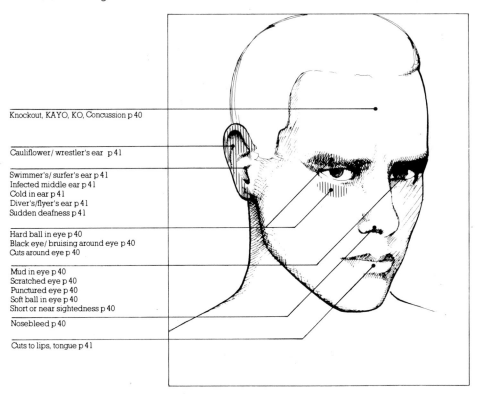

Knockout, KAYO, KO, Concussion p 40

Cauliflower/ wrestler's ear p 41

Swimmer's/ surfer's ear p 41
Infected middle ear p 41
Cold in ear p 41
Diver's/flyer's ear p 41
Sudden deafness p 41

Hard ball in eye p 40
Black eye/ bruising around eye p 40
Cuts around eye p 40

Mud in eye p 40
Scratched eye p 40
Punctured eye p 40
Soft ball in eye p 40
Short or near sightedness p 40

Nosebleed p 40

Cuts to lips, tongue p 41

Head

KNOCKOUT, KAYO, KO, CONCUSSION

Diagnosis: Victim has glazed eyes, is confused, cannot remember events up to and including accident.
Cause: Blow to head.
Treatment: *Self*—Follow first-aid advice. Remove any mouthguard or false teeth. Clear out mouth and nose to allow unobstructed breathing. *Then* remove from playing area to recover. *Medical*—See doctor.
Training: No training for 1 week minimum, depending on sport. Rugby Union advises no training or playing for at least 3 weeks, then return only after neurological exam; amateur boxing rules no fight for 28 days (1st KO), 84 days (2nd KO) or 1 year (3rd KO).

Eyes

Warning: If you wear glasses for sport, they must be unbreakable. Contact lenses will give good all-round vision. Many types of protective goggles (including ones that can be worn over glasses) are now available. Consult eye specialist.

MUD IN EYE

Treatment: *Self*—Wash eye out with water, or better, salt-water solution (1 teaspoon salt to 1 pint water), or eye drops.
Medical—Eyebath.

Training: Continue as usual. Use protective goggles where appropriate.

SCRATCHED EYE

Treatment: *Self*—Wash eye out with salt-water solution (1 teaspoon salt to 1 pint water). Cover with gauze pad. See doctor.
Medical—Antibiotic cream or drops.

PUNCTURED EYE

Treatment: *Self*—See doctor at once.
Medical—Remove foreign body.
Training: Continue as usual, using protective goggles or masks.
Warning: Check equipment regularly, especially fencing masks, etc.

SOFT BALL IN EYE

Particularly dangerous with small balls in squash, etc., which 'fit' eye socket.
Treatment: *Self*—Check for clouded vision, bruising. Seek medical advice.
Medical—Check eye lens. Check possible 'blow-out' fracture of eye-socket bones.
Training: Continue as usual. Wear protective goggles.
See: Squash (chapter 5).

HARD BALL IN EYE

Treatment: *Self*—Check that all eye movements up, down, side to side are normal, with no double or clouded vision. Check bones around eye for fracture. Apply icepack. Seek medical advice.

Medical—Check for clouded vision, fractures. Broken bone below eye can trap eye muscle, causing double vision later. Check eye lens.
Training: Continue as usual, wearing appropriate head and eye guards.

BLACK EYE/BRUISING AROUND EYE

Treatment: *Self*—Press icepack to affected area. Bruising may spread down beneath eye and even to other side over next 24–48 hr. Use enzyme cream after 48 hr.
Training: Continue as usual.

CUTS AROUND EYE

Treatment: *Self*—Press on edges of wound to stop bleeding. Draw edges together with adhesive plaster (adhesive bandage) or steristrip sutures (adhesive stitches).
Medical—As above. Surgical sutures.
See: Boxing (chapter 5).

SHORT OR NEAR SIGHTEDNESS

See: Boxing (chapter 5).

Nose

See: Flu, Hay fever, Head colds (chapter 1).

NOSEBLEED

Cause: Usually direct blow, sometimes infection.
Treatment: *Self*—Pinch nostrils together (immediately below bony part) for 5–10 min until blood clots. If bleeding

continues, see doctor.
Medical—Icepack.
Possibly adrenalin. Check
for nose fracture. Check
nasal passages are open.
Surgery if required,
antibiotics if cause is
infection.

Mouth and teeth
Warning: Never play
sports with false teeth in
place; if dislodged they
could cause choking.
Never chew gum for same
reason.
Always wear mouthguard
in sports where facial
blows are possible.
Nowadays these are light,
custom-made, comfortable
and inexpensive.

CUTS TO LIPS, TONGUE
Treatment: *Self*—Use ice
and compress if possible.
Medical—Stitches, but
usually heal easily without.

Ears

CAULIFLOWER/
WRESTLER'S EAR
Diagnosis: Swollen, painful
ear.
Cause: Blood seeps into
cartilage, which swells up,
due to blow or rubbing, as
in rugby scrum, boxing or
martial arts.
Treatment: *Self*—ICE;
compress firmly with
bandage around head.
After 48 hr use enzyme
cream.
Medical—Anti-inflammatory
drugs. Occasionally
drainage. Later, plastic
surgery.

Training: Continue as usual.
Can be prevented in some
sports by wearing helmet
or using tape around ears.

SWIMMER'S/SURFER'S
EAR
Diagnosis: Earache or
soreness in outer ear canal
suffered by swimmers,
surfers. Waggling ear hurts.
Cause: Persistent wetness.
Reaction to salt, chlorine.
Repeated rubbing or
scratching of ear.
Treatment: *Self*—Dry well.
Prevent by using ear plugs,
drop of olive oil in ears
before long session in water.
Medical—Antibiotic/
cortisone ear drops.

INFECTED MIDDLE
EAR
Diagnosis: Pain deep in
ear. Waggling outer ear
does *not* hurt. Temperature
may be raised. Sticky, smelly
discharge may appear.
Cause: Infection of eardrum
and middle ear. May be
due to tooth, mouth or throat
infection.
Treatment: *Self*—
Painkillers.
Medical—Antibiotics.
Training: Continue
exercise on land. Do not
swim until given
permission by doctor. If
'grommets' have been put
in, check with doctor.

COLD IN EAR
Diagnosis: Fuzzy hearing,
maybe pain, especially
when flying or diving.
Crackles and pops but no
temperature.
Cause: Glue-like mucus
from cold in middle ear

clogs eardrum.
Treatment: *Self*—'Pop' ears
by holding nose then
swallowing hard
repeatedly with mouth
closed. Chew gum. Blow up
balloons. Breathe in
menthol inhalation.
Medical—Nasal and ear
decongestants.
Training: Avoid sudden
changes in pressure
(diving, flying).

DIVER'S/FLYER'S EAR
Diagnosis: Pain in ear due
to change of air pressure
when diving, subaqua
diving, flying, etc.

Treat as for Cold in ear.

SUDDEN DEAFNESS
Diagnosis: Really does
occur all of a sudden,
sometimes accompanied
by dizziness.
Cause: Ruptured drum in
middle ear from too loud a
noise, sudden severe
increase in pressure (as in
high diving, subaqua
diving); occasionally
disease of arteries in
elderly. Occurs
cumulatively in shooting if
proper ear muffs or plugs
not used.
Treatment: *Self*—See
doctor within 48 hr.
Medical—Surgical repair
of drum.
Training: Continue as usual,
but ensure proper ear
protection (shooting); clear
catarrh before diving using
menthol crystals, but do not
overuse potent nosedrops
(max. 4 days use). No
swimming until cleared by
doctor.

Neck and shoulder

Possibly the weakest link in the body and yet the least well trained. All the vital connections between the head and body pass through this area and a fractured neck can mean permanent paralysis. But even now, international Rugby Union footballers (mimicked by youngsters) practise 'dropping the scrum'. 'In the name of sport I paralyse you' is hardly a maxim to be proud of. Tragic college and pro football accidents are also not uncommon in the United States.

Warning: Neck pains after heavy fall, car crash, etc., **must** be checked by doctor (see also Head warning, p 39).

Head hanger's neck p 43
Arthritis of neck p 43

Disc or facet joint pain p 43

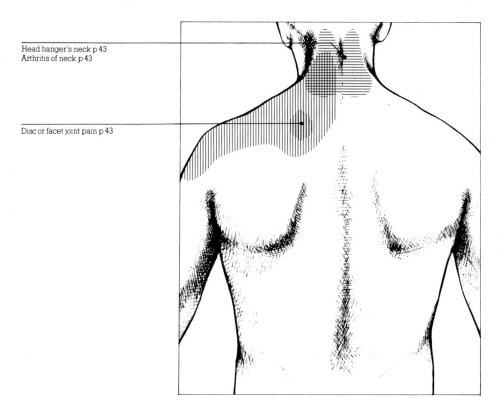

HEAD HANGER'S NECK

Diagnosis: Although neck can be moved in all directions, it aches, especially looking up and down.

Cause: Strain on muscles and ligaments attached to bottom of skull, especially from jobs which involve typing, drawing, etc., all day.

Treatment: *Self*—Warmth. Massage. Avoid thrusting head forward. If possible, raise desk or typewriter so head and neck and upper body are held straighter. Correct posture (see Back, p 64). Painkillers.
Medical—Ultrasound. Short-wave diathermy. Cortisone injection.

Training: Normal general fitness routine.

ARTHRITIS OF NECK (CERVICAL SPONDYLITIS/ SPONDYLOSIS OF NECK)

Diagnosis: *All* neck movements painfree until limit of range is reached on one or both sides. Test as shown in diagrams. (Check also Disc or facet joint pain.)

Cause: Arthritis. May be disease-type but usually of the 'wear and tear' variety.

Treatment: *Self*— Painkillers. Exercise neck regularly with slow, gentle 'nodding', stretching backwards and forwards and from side to side, and turning left and right.
Medical—Anti-inflammatory drugs. Short-wave diathermy. Traction. Manipulation.

Training: Normal general fitness routine but avoid games that involve violent twisting of neck (rugby, American football, wrestling). Sports involving overhead arm action may have problems (in tennis, badminton; for baseball catcher, cricket fielder, etc.).

DISC OR FACET JOINT PAIN

Diagnosis: Range of neck movements limited and painful (but not *all* movements painful). Test as shown in diagrams.

Exaggerated 'nodding' and 'side-to-side' movements can also bring on pain in shoulder, arm, hand, back or chest.

Cause: Neck twisted, in sport or even sleeping (but *not* 'sitting in a draught'!). Bones in neck move out of proper alignment.

Treatment: *Self*— Painkillers. Wide, self-supportive collar of newspaper wrapped in scarf then tied firmly around neck. At night, tie loop around centre of pillow to make butterfly shape which will support head.
Medical—Manipulation. Traction. Soft or plastic collar. Painkillers and muscle relaxants. Pain down arm with evidence of weak muscles can continue 4–8 weeks whatever treatment used—be patient!

Training: Avoid twisting head; otherwise normal general fitness routine unless it brings on pain. Bike routine recommended (p 103).

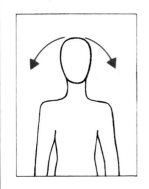 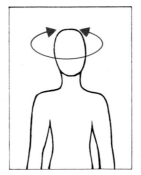 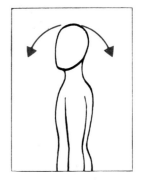

Neck and chest

This is where the heart and lungs live and therefore potentially the most dangerous area for self-diagnosis. While recent sports activity might *seem* to relate to a sudden pain here, other problems may be the cause.

Warning: Constant pain in centre or left side of chest, especially if also felt in arms, neck and/or back, needs urgent medical attention—particularly if combined with shortness of breath, cold sweat or fatigue.

Stabbing pain when breathing in: check with doctor, as this could be result of lung infection or injured ribs or spine.

NB If you have a temperature **stop all training**. No *sporting* injury (apart from dehydration) makes your temperature rise. Resume training only when feeling completely well again.

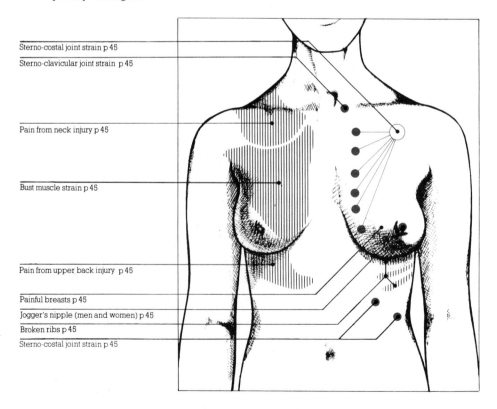

Sterno-costal joint strain p 45

Sterno-clavicular joint strain p 45

Pain from neck injury p 45

Bust muscle strain p 45

Pain from upper back injury p 45

Painful breasts p 45

Jogger's nipple (men and women) p 45

Broken ribs p 45

Sterno-costal joint strain p 45

PAIN FROM NECK INJURY

Carry out diagnostic tests for Neck and shoulder injuries (pp 42–3).

PAIN FROM UPPER BACK INJURY

Carry out diagnostic tests for Back injuries (pp 60–4).

STERNO-CLAVICULAR JOINT STRAIN

Diagnosis: Bony knob at top and side of breastbone tender to pressure; pain may travel up front of neck towards ear. All shoulder movements cause pain in bony knob.
Cause: Strain on joint where collar- and breastbones meet.
Treatment: *Self*—Painkillers. Rest arm. *Medical*—Anti-inflammatory drugs. Ultrasound. Cortisone injection.
Training: Normal general fitness routine; avoid using arm until tenderness goes.

STERNO-COSTAL JOINT STRAIN

Diagnosis: Tender to pressure over rib joints, 5 cm (2 in) approx. from midline of breastbone; may even feel like lump (as in women's breasts) or cause pain breathing deeply in and out, slouching, twisting or turning. Pain may occur on one or both sides.
Cause: Strain on hinge joint of rib with breastbone.
Treatment: *Self*—Painkillers. Rest. Avoid being crushed. May take time to heal and can reoccur. *Medical*—Anti-inflammatory

drugs. Ultrasound. Cortisone injections.
Training: Normal general fitness routine, but avoid press-ups, weight-training with arms.

BUST MUSCLE STRAIN (PECTORALIS)

Diagnosis: Muscles tender to touch, especially at top front of arm. Elbows out, push hands together across chest; pain confirmed in bust muscles.

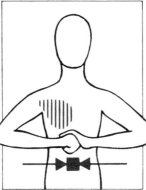

Cause: Severe strain, often in martial arts.
Treatment: *Self*—ICE. Avoid lifting and carrying heavy objects with elbows out (as in lifting a tray). Stretching—see exercise 7. *Medical*—Ultrasound. Cross-frictional massage.
Training: Normal general fitness routine. Isometric exercise against other hand as in diagnostic test. See muscle ladder (p 104), with press-ups—pull-ups.

JOGGER'S NIPPLE (MEN AND WOMEN)

Diagnosis: Sore or bleeding nipples.
Cause: Rubbing of clothing on unprotected nipple

(male or female); common in distance running, jogging.
Treatment: *Self*—Leave to heal naturally; allow air to get to affected part if possible, otherwise cover with adhesive plaster/bandage. Prevent by using petroleum jelly or tape with shiny adhesive plaster (smooth plastic adhesive strip) before running; wear clean top.

PAINFUL BREASTS

Diagnosis: Painful.
Cause: Bouncing, unsupported breasts may be painful after exercise due to friction (see Jogger's nipple) or torn tissue. Blows to breast do not cause cancer; damaged breast fat, however, is very tender, may feel like lump and takes time to heal. Check with doctor.

BROKEN RIBS

Diagnosis: Tender after squeezing injured area with hands, compressing and releasing ribs rapidly. Most common area shown in diagram, but pain may be felt elsewhere.
Cause: Crushing or heavy blow.
Treatment: *Self*—Painkillers. Avoid movements that produce pain. Strapping may be more trouble than it's worth. Takes about 4–6 weeks to heal. Seek medical attention if increasing shortness of breath or coughing up blood. *Medical*—As above. X-ray.
Training: Continue as usual if pain tolerable.

Shoulder

This joint has a wide range of movements whose essential strength depends on muscles and ligaments. People often take up activities such as throwing, playing badminton or house-decorating without any thought of the problems of acute overuse. Vital nerves and blood vessels are close by the area, in the armpit.

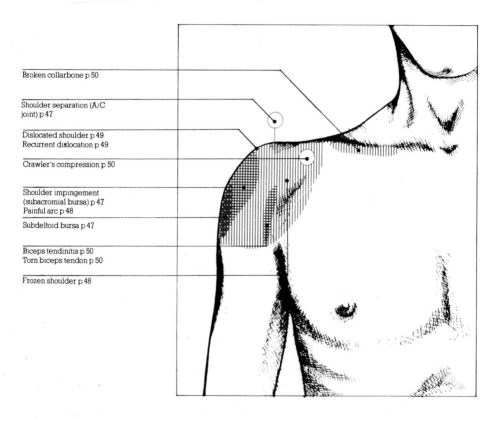

Broken collarbone p 50

Shoulder separation (A/C joint) p 47

Dislocated shoulder p 49
Recurrent dislocation p 49

Crawler's compression p 50

Shoulder impingement
(subacromial bursa) p 47
Painful arc p 48

Subdeltoid bursa p 47

Biceps tendinitis p 50
Torn biceps tendon p 50

Frozen shoulder p 48

SHOULDER SEPARATION (ACROMIO-CLAVICULAR JOINT—A/C JOINT)

Diagnosis: Hurts when top of shoulder pressed; may have visible 'step' in shoulder. Hurts to throw or bowl overarm (cricket). Complete separation may produce fewer problems later than slight separation.

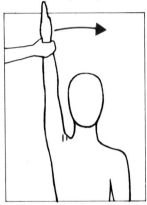

(a) Move raised arm in towards head; pain confirmed in shoulder joint.

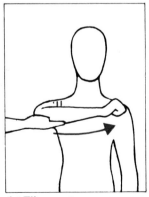

(b) Elbow out, move arm up across chest; pain confirmed in shoulder joint.
Cause: Sprain or rupture of joint ligaments between collarbone and top of shoulder.

Treatment: *Self*—Rest. If pain severe, put arm in sling. Avoid carrying heavy weights. Move only within painfree range.
Medical—Anti-inflammatory drugs. Mobilization. Cortisone injection. Surgery.
Training: Normal general fitness routine, but avoid throwing overarm, all overhead work and press-ups.
See: Badminton, Baseball, Basketball, Cricket, Cycling, Equestrian sports, Football (American), Handball, Netball, Rugby, Squash, Tennis, Volleyball (chapter 5).

SUBDELTOID BURSA

Diagnosis: Arm must be tested (i.e. arm movement blocked) between 45° and horizontal to confirm pain.

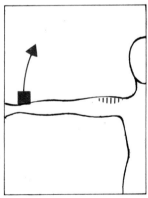

Cause: Overuse.
Treatment: *Self*—ICE. Rest. Aspirin.
Medical—Ultrasound. Cortisone injection.
Training: Avoid training that flares injury, e.g. gymnastics fixed cross, press-ups.
See: Tennis (chapter 5).

SHOULDER IMPINGEMENT (SUBACROMIAL BURSA)

Diagnosis: Pain occurs when extended arm is brought sideways to vertical (especially last 20°). Hurts to throw

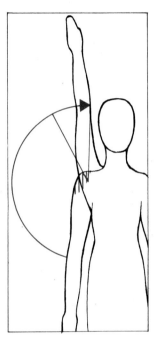

overarm. Often accompanies other shoulder problems. If diagnosis does not reveal pain but hard overarm throwing hurts and bowling (cricket) overarm does not, probably subacromial bursa problem.
Cause: Trapping of bursa or 'grease bag' between armbone and shoulder tip.
Treatment: *Self*—Rest. Aspirin.
Medical—Anti-inflammatory drugs. Cortisone injection.

Shortwave diathermy.
Training: Normal general fitness routine, but avoid overhead work. Do not throw overarm; instead throw side or underarm, or 'bowl' ball.
See: Badminton, Baseball, Basketball, Cricket, Handball, Netball, Squash, Swimming, Tennis, Volleyball (chapter 5).

FROZEN SHOULDER

Diagnosis: Pain and restricted movement in shoulder joint.
Cause: Wrenched shoulder. Overuse in 50+ age group. Often accompanied by painful 'arc' problems in young.
Treatment: *Self*— Immediate support in sling for 48 hr. ICE. Aspirin. Later, remobilize shoulder gently. Maintain finger and wrist movements at all times.
Medical—Shortwave diathermy. Physiotherapy and mobilization. Cortisone injection. Anti-inflammatory drugs. Surgical manipulation.
Training: Normal general fitness routine, but swimming and running may be painful; patience needed as joint will flare again if cure not complete. Eventually, graded shoulder strengthening needed.
NB Full recovery can take two years, though this may be shortened by medical treatment. Pain decreases but so does mobility, until shoulder is painfree but 'frozen'. Shoulder then has

to be slowly remobilized. Diabetics take longer to recover.

PAINFUL ARC

Diagnosis: Pain may occur in any of the following movements: when extended arm is lifted sideways to vertical, when this movement is blocked,

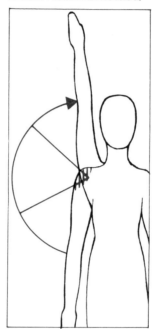

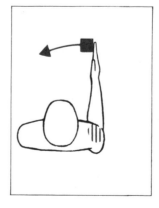

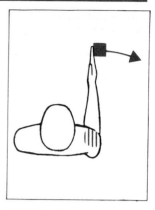

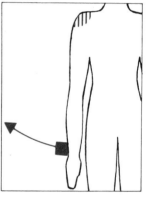

and when arm is out in front and movement left or right is blocked. Pain occurs in *arc* between 80 and 110°.
Cause: Overuse of any of three shoulder muscles or poor blood supply in 50+ age group. Painting ceilings or similar action often triggers pain.
Treatment: *Self*—Rest. Avoid lifting and carrying heavy objects with elbows out (as in lifting a tray). NB Diabetics usually take much longer to heal.
Medical—Deep friction massage. Ultrasound. Cortisone injection. Complications (such as calcium in tendon, rupture)

may need surgery.
Training: Normal general
fitness routine. Keep arms
in trim by using spring-type
chest-expander—follow
muscle ladder principle.
See: Badminton, Basketball,
Handball, Netball, Squash,
Swimming, Volleyball
(chapter 5).

DISLOCATED SHOULDER

Diagnosis: Shoulder looks
square; arm cannot be
lifted outwards from side.
Also, see Recurrent
dislocation of shoulder.

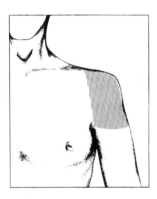

Cause: Severe wrench as
armbone dislocated from
shoulder socket.
Treatment: *Self*—**Do not
fiddle**! Put in sling. Seek
medical advice as fractures
may complicate injury.
Medical—Reset under
anaesthetic. Sling.
Training: Keep shoulder
immobilized. Heels (see
p 112, step 6). Bicycle,
running, rowing/rowing
machine. Later swimming.
When fully mobile again,
begin strengthening of
shoulder muscles.

RECURRENT DISLOCATION OF SHOULDER

In some people, the
shoulder dislocates easily
and often, especially in
contact sports. It can also
be relocated quite easily.
Treatment: *Self*—1 Lie face
down on couch/table. Let
injured arm hang down
holding heavy weight.
2 Standing up, manipulate
into place using what is
known as Kocher

manoeuvre (see diagram).
If this doesn't work first
time, don't fiddle, see
doctor.
Medical—Put in place.
Surgery can prevent further
dislocation by tightening
muscles and ligaments.
Training: Normal general
fitness routine once
shoulder back in place.
Avoid falling on shoulder or
above-shoulder racquet
work until soreness gone.
Build up shoulder strength.

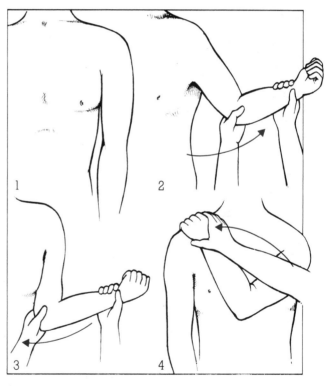

BICEPS TENDINITIS
Diagnosis: Palm up, try to lift forearm. Pain confirmed in front of shoulder.

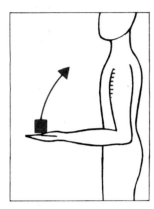

Cause: Overuse of muscle due to carrying, lifting or pulling with elbow bent.
Treatment: *Self*—ICE. Rest. Aspirin. After 48 hr use frictional massage on tender spot.
Medical—Deep friction massage. Ultrasound. Cortisone injection.
Training: Normal general fitness routine. Follow muscle ladder principle. Avoid pulling or carrying with bent elbow. Build gradually into chin-ups.
See: Canoeing/kayaking (chapter 5).

TORN BICEPS TENDON (POPEYE ARM)
Diagnosis: As for Biceps tendinitis but accompanied by bruising. Even when relaxed, muscle looks bunched (like Popeye's!).
Cause: In older people, lifting too heavy weight with elbow bent. In younger people, sudden check when lifting heavy weight or making full-blooded move with bent elbow (in wrestling, weightlifting, etc.).
Treatment: *Self*—ICE. Rest. After 1 week start easy stretching to straighten elbow.
Medical—Ultrasound. Stretching. As torn ends of tendon usually reattach further down, surgery rarely required.
Training: Normal general fitness routine. Follow muscle ladder principle. Build up to chin-ups.

BROKEN COLLARBONE
Diagnosis: Victim feels bones rubbing together even if break not obviously visible.
Cause: Blow on collarbone or fall.
Treatment: *Self*—Put arm on injured side in sling. See doctor.
Medical—Sling. Occasionally surgery.
Training: Normal general fitness routine. Use bicycle one-handed (static bike recommended!). Pattering (see p 101), then running; make sure calf, thigh and stomach muscles are kept in shape. Shoulder and hand mobility must be maintained at all times. Supporting elbow on injured side with opposite hand, wave forearm from side to side. 6–8 weeks required for bones to knit.

CRAWLER'S COMPRESSION
See: Swimming (chapter 5).

Elbow

Lack of coordination and overuse produce the majority of injuries in the elbow, which, with associated muscles, also controls wrist and finger movements. Many sports have their own names for particular injuries, but even tennis elbow can be caused by using a screwdriver! Baseball's pitcher's elbow actually covers several different injuries, all caused by different pitching techniques. Often correction of the technical fault by a good coach cures the injury.

Warning: Children who injure this joint may suffer distorted or slow growth, as their bones are still soft. Medical treatment is essential.

Emergency: Persistent 'pins and needles' in the hand below a recently injured elbow or lack of pulse at the wrist are danger signals. Seek medical treatment at once.

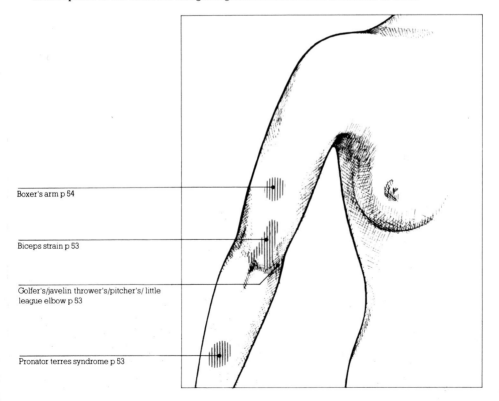

Boxer's arm p 54

Biceps strain p 53

Golfer's/javelin thrower's/pitcher's/ little
league elbow p 53

Pronator terres syndrome p 53

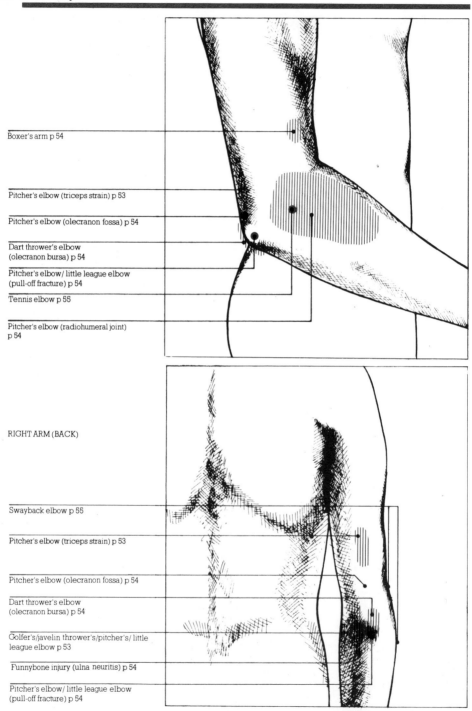

Boxer's arm p 54

Pitcher's elbow (triceps strain) p 53

Pitcher's elbow (olecranon fossa) p 54

Dart thrower's elbow
(olecranon bursa) p 54

Pitcher's elbow/ little league elbow
(pull-off fracture) p 54

Tennis elbow p 55

Pitcher's elbow (radiohumeral joint)
p 54

RIGHT ARM (BACK)

Swayback elbow p 55

Pitcher's elbow (triceps strain) p 53

Pitcher's elbow (olecranon fossa) p 54

Dart thrower's elbow
(olecranon bursa) p 54

Golfer's/javelin thrower's/pitcher's/ little
league elbow p 53

Funnybone injury (ulna neuritis) p 54

Pitcher's elbow/ little league elbow
(pull-off fracture) p 54

BICEPS STRAIN
Diagnosis: With palm up, try to bend elbow. Pain confirmed in elbow or upper arm.

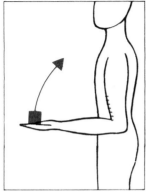

Cause: Strain on biceps muscle (bulging one on front of arm, above elbow).
Treatment: *Self*—Rest. ICE. Slow to heal on its own. Avoid lifting heavy loads. *Medical*—Ultrasound. Frictional massage.
Training: Normal general fitness routine, including upper body strength; *no* forearm bends or pull-ups.
See: Archery (chapter 5).

PRONATOR TERRES SYNDROME
Diagnosis: Gripping friend's hand, try to turn palm down. Resist pressure on tip of middle finger. Pain confirmed in forearm.
Cause: Technical fault in racquet sports.
Treatment: *Self*—Rest. ICE. Pain may persist for several months. Stretch forearm muscle by forcing tips of fingers back until pain felt in forearm. Hold, release and repeat.
Medical—Cortisone

injection. Surgery.
Training: Continue as usual unless painful.
See: Squash, Tennis (chapter 5).

GOLFER'S/JAVELIN THROWER'S/PITCHER'S/LITTLE LEAGUE ELBOW
All occur on or around bony knob on *inner* side of elbow. Although injury appears to be produced by different actions, it is forceful curl of wrist that puts undue stress on elbow.
Diagnosis: With palm up, resist wrist curl. Pain confirmed round bony knob on *inner* side of elbow. Also, try to force open closed fist.

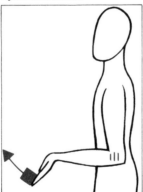

Cause: Strain of forearm muscle's tendon at elbow. These muscles curl wrist and close fingers into fist. Powerful pulling and gripping may strain them and even pull off a piece of bone or damage 'growing point' in youngsters.
Treatment: *Self*—Rest. ICE. Avoid lifting weight with tightly gripping hand (i.e. hammering, pulling up weeds, lifting suitcase).

Stretch fingers backwards to start of pain, hold and release. Repeat.
Medical—Cross-frictional massage. Ultrasound. Anti-inflammatory drugs. Cortisone injections. Surgery.
Training: Normal general fitness routine, including upper body strength; *no* grip strengthening, *no* wrist curls.
See: Golf, Baseball, Track and field athletics (chapter 5).

PITCHER'S ELBOW (TRICEPS STRAIN)
Diagnosis: Palm up, resist attempt to push forearm down to side.

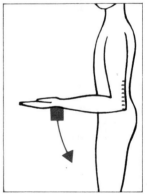

Cause: Too much load on elbow in, say, 'clean' segment of clean and jerk weightlifting. Forceful straightening of elbow, as in throwing, or serving in tennis.
Treatment: *Self*—Rest. ICE. Recovers quite quickly. *Medical*—Ultrasound. Cross-frictional massage. Anti-inflammatory drugs. Cortisone injection.
Training: Normal general

fitness routine, *no* heavy weights until painfree.
See: Baseball, Tennis (chapter 5).

PITCHER'S ELBOW (OLECRANON FOSSA)

Diagnosis: Straighten elbow; pain felt when it locks. No pain when bent.
Cause: Repeatedly snapping elbow straight, as in throwing or in karate chop.
Treatment: *Self*—Rest. ICE. *Medical*—Ultrasound. Cortisone injection.
Training: Normal fitness routine. Maintain movement but avoid 100 per cent 'snap' of throw. When pain is no longer felt on straightening elbow, ease back to full throwing. Take your time, as problem may flare up again.
See: Baseball (chapter 5).

DART THROWER'S ELBOW (OLECRANON BURSA)

Diagnosis: Tender swelling round tip of elbow.
Cause: Repeated flexing of elbow, not necessarily with heavy weight; or leaning on elbow as in postmatch beer drinking; or rifle shooting; or gout; or infection, often grazed elbow, etc.; or fall.
Treatment: *Self*—Rest. ICE. Avoid pressure on elbow. If in doubt about infection, see doctor.
Medical—Antibiotics if infected; anti-inflammatory drugs (also for gout); drain fluid; cortisone injection.
Training: Normal training routine; avoid any

exercises that cause more pain in elbow.
See: Darts (chapter 5).

PITCHER'S ELBOW/LITTLE LEAGUE ELBOW (PULL-OFF FRACTURE)

Diagnosis: Arm out, palm up, try to push down by side. Pain confirmed on bony tip of elbow.
Cause: Muscle tears away from bone taking small fragment with it.
Treatment: *Self*—Rest. ICE. Allow some 8 weeks for fragment to reattach. *Medical*—Splinting. Possible surgery.
Training: Normal fitness routine; consult medical adviser.
See: Baseball (chapter 5).

PITCHER'S ELBOW (RADIOHUMERAL JOINT)

Diagnosis: As for Tennis elbow, **plus** passive straightening of elbow, or full bending of elbow and full twisting of forearm (from palm up to palm down and vice versa).
Cause: Snapping elbow straight as wrist turns palm down (as in badminton shot at net) sprains joint.
Treatment: *Self*—Rest. ICE. Needs more time to heal than tennis elbow. *Medical*—Shortwave diathermy. Anti-inflammatory drugs. Cortisone injection. All concurrent with tennis elbow treatment.
Training: Normal fitness routine. If uncomplicated by tennis elbow, all moves

that do not produce pain. Make sure technique is correct.
See: Badminton, Baseball, Tennis (chapter 5).

BOXER'S ARM

Diagnosis: Fist clenched, thumb on top, try to lift forearm. Pain confirmed in upper arm.

Cause: Small spur of bone that develops in some boxers just above elbow is broken off by direct blow.
Treatment: *Self*—Rest. ICE. With extended rest (4–6 weeks), spur will reattach itself.
Medical—Ultrasound. Cortisone injections. Surgical removal.
Training: Normal fitness routine, including upper body strength; *no* punching until painfree.

FUNNYBONE INJURY (ULNA NEURITIS)

Diagnosis: Straightening (flattening) elbow completely then touching spot behind (inside) elbow knob produces tingling; pain, 'pins and needles' down forearm, classically into 4th and 5th fingers. Pain may even extend upwards into shoulder, causing wakefulness at night.

Cause: Pressure/damage to nerve; by blow, leaning on it or overuse of nearby muscles.

Treatment: *Self*—Rest. ICE. Avoid pressure on nerve, especially from table edge, car window.

Medical—EMG. Cortisone injection. Surgery.

Training: Normal fitness routine. Seek medical advice.

SWAYBACK ELBOW

See: Gymnastics (chapter 5).

TENNIS ELBOW

The most common injury to this joint. Although labelled a tennis complaint, it occurs in any sport where the elbow is constantly bending while the hand is gripping, e.g. canoeing, kayaking, badminton, baseball pitching, tenpin bowling, even flyfishing. While much has been written about the condition, its cause is simple. You have been asking your forearm muscles to do too much! This often happens as you improve at a sport, say when you add curve or spin to your throw or stroke. If you do not also increase your body's strength to handle this, the result is an injury. Pain and tenderness to the touch occur on the outer side of the elbow and may extend down the forearm. Turning the hand palm up, cocking the wrist

and straightening the fingers all cause pain.

Diagnosis: See drawings below.

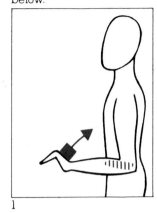

1

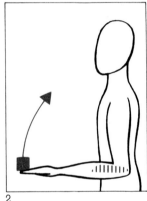

2

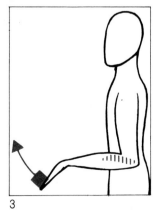

3

1 Resist cocking wrist backwards. Pain confirmed.
2 Fingers extended, palm down, try to lift forearm with resistance over tips of fingers.
3 Fingers extended downwards, resist cocking wrist at fingertips.

Cause: Classic 'overuse' strain where hand drops, wrist twists and arm bends—anything from using screwdriver to tennis. Forearm muscles are not strong enough to take strain. Often caused by technical fault or unsuitable equipment.

See also: Radiohumeral joint sprain (for complications).

Treatment: *Self*—Rest. ICE. Avoid lifting *all* objects with palm down. Even writing with thin pen/pencil causes flare-up. Use thicker pen grip, or grip between index and 3rd fingers, Chinese-style. Long-handled screwdrivers reduce force required.

Medical—Ultrasound. Deep friction massage. Cortisone injection. Surgery.

Training: Normal fitness routine. When painfree, strengthen forearm with supported wrist curls. (With elbow supported, raise and lower wrist while holding 2 kg (4½ lb) weight.)

Extra aids: Forearm strapping and tennis elbow supports; these act like 'outer skeleton' and take load off sore spot.

See: Archery, Badminton, Baseball, Canoeing, Golf, Skiing, Squash (chapter 5).

Wrist and hand

A large area of the brain is reserved to look after this sensitive and vital part, which can handle an activity as delicate as sewing yet act as a weapon in martial arts. As a first-line sensor it comes into contact with objects that may damage and interfere with its fine control. And its many bones may suffer strains and sprains.

Warning: There are so many bones and joints in fingers and wrists that self-diagnosis of a sprain or break is difficult. Seek medical advice.

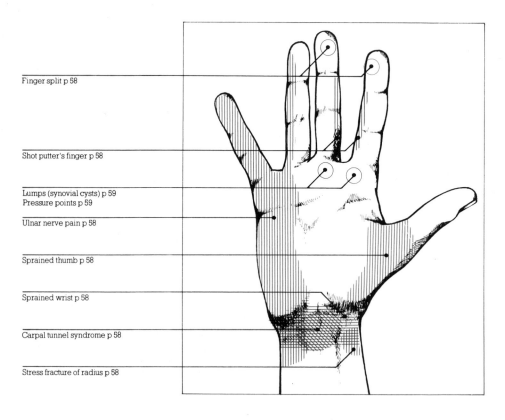

Finger split p 58

Shot putter's finger p 58

Lumps (synovial cysts) p 59
Pressure points p 59

Ulnar nerve pain p 58

Sprained thumb p 58

Sprained wrist p 58

Carpal tunnel syndrome p 58

Stress fracture of radius p 58

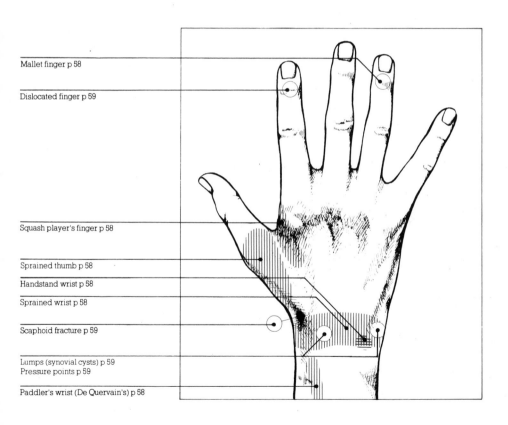

Mallet finger p 58

Dislocated finger p 59

Squash player's finger p 58

Sprained thumb p 58

Handstand wrist p 58

Sprained wrist p 58

Scaphoid fracture p 59

Lumps (synovial cysts) p 59
Pressure points p 59

Paddler's wrist (De Quervain's) p 58

SPRAINED WRIST

Diagnosis: Moving wrist in any direction painful; pain shows up sometimes in small, sometimes in larger movements.

Cause: Usually twist or fall, spraining linings and ligaments.

Treatment: *Self*—ICE. Strap using 1–2 in stretch elastic bandage (wrist in 'cocked' position, make tight fist, relax it, then strap wrist in that position); when better use elastic wrist support. Aspirin. Continue painfree wrist movements. *Medical*—As above. Anti-inflammatory drugs. Shortwave diathermy.

Training: Normal general fitness routine. Wrist movement should be supported 2–4 weeks. Work up to, not through pain.

STRESS FRACTURE OF RADIUS

See: Gymnastics (chapter 5).

PADDLER'S WRIST (DE QUERVAIN'S)

See: Canoeing, Rowing (chapter 5).

SPRAINED THUMB

Diagnosis: Tip of thumb can be moved but lower joints hurt on all movements, especially pushing outwards. May show swelling and bruising.

Cause: Forceful wrenching of lower thumb joint.

Warning: If bones fracture so thumb is displaced, surgery (pinning) will be necessary.

Treatment: *Self*—ICE (compression essential). Strap from wrist down to sore joint with 1–2 in elastic support, covering palm also; high sling helps reduce swelling over 48 hr. Anti-bruise cream. Unstrap after 48 hr and gently try opening fist, then closing with fingers over thumb; rebandage. Support thumb 4–6 weeks if any possibility of it being bent backwards. *Medical*—Anti-inflammatory drugs and cream. Ultrasound. Enzyme creams after 48 hr.

Training: Normal general fitness routine; support thumb if necessary. Avoid large ball-handling games (football, basketball), martial arts.

SHOT PUTTER'S FINGER

See: Track and field athletics (chapter 5).

SQUASH PLAYER'S FINGER

See: Squash (chapter 5).

ULNAR NERVE PAIN

Diagnosis: Pins and needles or pain down 4th and 5th fingers.

Cause: Nerve pain. See: Elbow (p 54).

CARPAL TUNNEL SYNDROME

Diagnosis: Pain in palm, thumb, index and middle fingers; sometimes in wrist, forearm and upper arm. Pain sufficient to wake you at night. Tapping wrist on palm side creases may cause shooting sensation in hand. Thumb muscles may weaken.

Cause: Pressure on nerve passing into wrist, from overuse, pregnancy or disease (e.g. underactive thyroid).

Treatment: *Self*—ICE. Keep wrist higher than elbow. Seek medical advice. *Medical*—'Water' tablets. Cortisone injection. Surgery. Correct thyroid problems.

Training: Continue as usual unless painful. Repeated pressure may flare condition.

FINGER SPLIT

Diagnosis: Split in skin.

Cause: Overuse. Grip prevents finger sliding, pressure causes split in skin. Usually occurs with stick or racquet sports.

Treatment: *Self*—Tape before training or playing.

MALLET FINGER

Diagnosis: Inability to straighten last joint of finger.

Cause: Tendon that straightens tip of finger torn off.

Treatment: *Self*—ICE. Use pencil or short piece of wood as splint under finger. Strap so last joint straight. Seek medical advice. *Medical*—Splint.

Training: Continue as usual, if possible with splint in place.

HANDSTAND WRIST

Diagnosis: Back of wrist

aches when hand forced back, as in handstand.
Cause: Inadequate wrist flexibility.
Treatment: *Self*—Do not overwork wrist; gradually build up handstands, press-ups. Try turning hands outwards or inwards during handstands. Rest. *Medical*—Rest. Shortwave diathermy.
Training: Continue as usual, but build up handstand work gradually.

SCAPHOID FRACTURE
Diagnosis: Pain in hollow between two thumb tendons on back of wrist.
Cause: Fall onto hand.
Treatment: *Self*—Seek medical advice.
Medical—Difficult to diagnose even with X-ray (may need scan). Plaster cast. Splint.
Training: Continue as usual, if possible with plaster cast.

DISLOCATED FINGER
Diagnosis: Tip of finger points backwards. Lump in front of end joint.
Treatment:
Self—**Warning:** Only applicable to end joint—any others, seek medical help.
1 As soon as possible, pull, as if trying to stretch fingertip out from rest of finger; joint will slide back into place.
2 If unsuccessful, **stop**, seek medical help.
3 Strap injured finger to next finger for 24 hr.
4 Aspirin.
5 After 24 hr, gently move finger towards making a fist (warming in hot water, wearing protective rubber glove, may help).
6 Swelling may continue for months.
Medical—As for self-treatment.
Training: Continue as usual, but strap joint for 3 weeks

for ball-handling or martial arts sports.

LUMPS
Diagnosis: Hard or rubbery lumps, usually on back of wrist, can be on any finger or wrist joint. 95 per cent of lumps are synovial cysts.
Cause: Weak lining to joint bulges with yellow, jelly-like, joint-lubricating fluid.
Treatment: *Self*—Leave alone.
Medical—Pressure. Drain with needle. Surgery.
Training: Continue as usual.

PRESSURE POINTS
Diagnosis: Area tender to pressure or use, usually on back or outside of wrist.
Cause: Weakness in joint linings.
Treatment: *Self*—Bandage wrist firmly for training or playing.

Back

Walking on two legs has permitted us to develop those mechanical marvels the hands, but has also loaded our backs in the upright position. However, the concern with posture and deportment is negligible, even though more working days are lost to industry from back trouble than any other cause. Correct posture together with back and stomach muscle strength can save many aggravating days of pain.

As well as covering the diagnosis and treatment of back problems, this section includes some general tips on living and training with them. Don't forget that back injuries may not always be the same; manipulation didn't work this time perhaps, but it may still be the best choice of treatment next time.

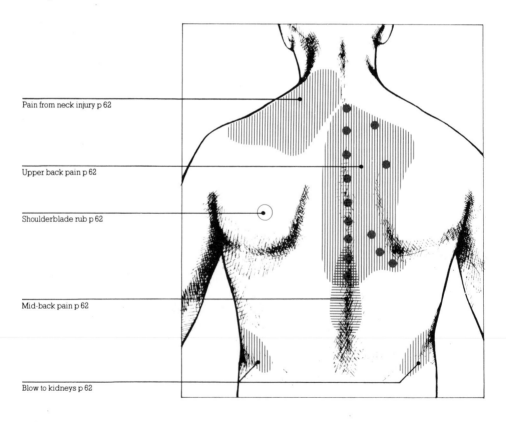

Pain from neck injury p 62

Upper back pain p 62

Shoulderblade rub p 62

Mid-back pain p 62

Blow to kidneys p 62

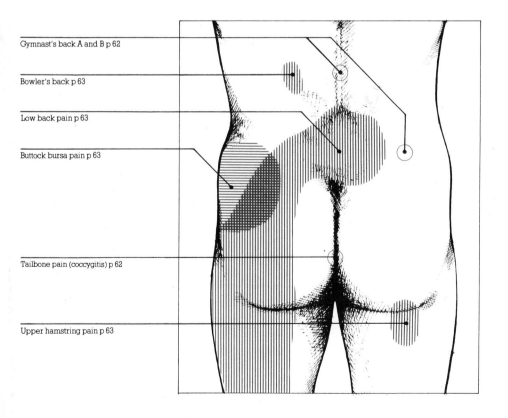

Gymnast's back A and B p 62

Bowler's back p 63

Low back pain p 63

Buttock bursa pain p 63

Tailbone pain (coccygitis) p 62

Upper hamstring pain p 63

UPPER BACK (DORSAL) PAIN

Diagnosis: Some or all of the following may produce pain: breathing or coughing; occasional movement of pain from back round to front; lowering chin onto chest; turning upper body one way rather than another. Bending to side probably produces no pain.

Cause: Backbone (facet joint) or 'shock absorber' in between (disc) moved out of place, so ligaments are stretched and muscles may cramp.

Treatment: *Self*—Rest. Seek medical advice. Avoid twisting top half of body and lifting from side. Instead, turn to face object before lifting. Sitting may be easier than lying down, so prop up pillows to form 'chairback' on bed. Painkillers. Always use back strain position. (See p 64.)
Medical—Rest. Painkillers. Manipulation.
Training: Normal general fitness routine, as long as painfree. Bicycling probably easier than running or swimming. No upper body work until better. Otherwise, general training for back (p. 65).
See: Golf, Rowing, Rugby (chapter 5).

MID-BACK PAIN

Diagnosis: Pain may be in loin area, as for Upper back, or when leaning backwards.
Cause: Pushing/pulling with rounded back.

Treatment: *Self*—Correct bad posture; use back strain position (see p 64) for life. Rest. Painkillers. Seek medical advice.
Medical—X-ray in teenagers (may be growth problem). Manipulation. Traction.
Training: Continue as usual if painfree. Maintain back strain position, especially with weights. Work on back strength when fit.
See: Rowing, Rugby (chapter 5).

SHOULDERBLADE RUB (SUB SCAPULAR CREPITUS)

Diagnosis: Shoulder tests (see: Shoulder) and twisting upper body do *not* produce pain. But circling shoulder (not arm) is painful and produces grating feeling if flat of hand is placed on shoulderblade.
Cause: Rough underside of shoulderblade rubbing over ribs.
Treatment: *Self*—Hold shoulders squarely; tense, rounded shoulders flare pain.
Medical—Shortwave diathermy. Cortisone injection under shoulderblade.
Training: Continue as usual. Ensure square shoulders.
See: Golf (chapter 5).

BLOW TO KIDNEYS

Treatment: Apply ice/cold compress to ease pain.
Training: Continue as normal, as much as pain allows.
NB If blood appears in urine, seek medical advice at once.

PAIN FROM NECK INJURY

Carry out diagnostic tests for Neck and shoulder injuries (pp 42–3).

Lower Back

GYMNAST'S BACK A

Diagnosis: Pain only when arching backwards.
Cause: Bones knocking on each other when back arched in acute angle (hyperextension).
Treatment: *Self*—See: Gymnastics (chapter 5).
Medical—Ultrasound. Cortisone injection. Rarely, surgery.
Training: See: Gymnastics.

GYMNAST'S BACK B

Diagnosis: Pain only in completion of full backwards arch. Swallows may hurt. Edge of pelvic bone on back tender to pressure, usually one side only.
Cause: Walkovers.
Treatment: *Self*—See: Gymnastics (chapter 5).
Medical—Ultrasound. Cortisone injection.
Training: See: Gymnastics.

TAILBONE PAIN (COCCYGITIS)

Diagnosis: Often constant pain, especially sitting down but sometimes bending forward. Tip of spine (bones between buttocks) tender to touch.
Cause: Sitting down suddenly and hard on tip of spine; may even cause fracture.
Treatment: *Self*—Sit

forward on fleshy part of upper thighs. Sit on inflatable ring or on gap between 2 cushions. Painkillers. Healing often takes more than 4 weeks—be patient! *Medical*—Painkillers. Anti-inflammatory drugs. Cortisone injection. Very rarely, surgery.
Training: Normal routine as far as possible, but avoid rowing and bicycling. It's only pain!
See: Skating (chapter 5).

UPPER HAMSTRING PAIN
See under: Upper leg, p 72.

BOWLER'S BACK
See: Cricket (chapter 5).

LOW BACK PAIN
There are many causes and medical advice should be sought, especially for teenage back problems. Fractures have not been covered.

BUTTOCK BURSA PAIN
Diagnosis: (a) Lie on stomach; pain in buttock muscles when straight leg raised. (b) Lying on front,

raise leg and block at position shown; pain at top of buttock.
Cause: Overwork makes grease bag under buttock muscle sore.
Treatment: *Self*—Rest. *Medical*—Ultrasound. Cortisone injection. Check circulation.
Training: Continue as usual; pain harmless but running may flare it.
Avoid stiff-kneed running style, sprints, hill-running, swinging straightened leg.

Mechanical problems
Diagnosis: Pain confirmed by some if not all of the following: coughing, sneezing, sitting, standing from sitting position, bending forward, backward, to *one* side, raising straight leg when lying flat on back.
Cause: Damaged disc or facet joint in spine.
Treatment: Rest will help but seek medical advice, *especially* for teenagers. Treatment may vary, even for same person on different occasions, so following are only guidelines:
Self—(a) Bedrest.
(b) Stretching: Hang from

arms 5–10 min (resting when necessary); using feet support straps, hang upside down, taking care getting into straps and not falling on your head!
(c) Self-manipulation (especially for niggling back ache, beginning of slow onset pain): Stand feet firmly and wide apart, turn upper body *towards* pain, put heel of hand over back wing of pelvis, gripping fingers with opposite hand, arch back, push pelvis forward *away* from pain and turn shoulders more towards back. Repeat several times, then throughout day.
(d) Sustained self-manipulation: Lie with painfree side on edge of bed, keep shoulders flat on bed, twist pelvis and leg on painful side up and over other leg to hang over edge, hold 15–20 min.
Medical—These are guidelines only; individual cases may need one or more treatments.
(a) Sudden onset of pain (may leave you unable to move): Manipulation; painkillers; rest.
(b) Slow onset of pain (gradual stiffening after gardening or long exercise): Rest; traction; painkillers; support corset.
(c) Sciatica (pain felt in leg, even down to foot, from disc pressing on spinal nerve): Rest; traction/ manipulation; painkillers; support corset.
(d) Sciatica with weak muscles (muscles weak due to nerve damage—

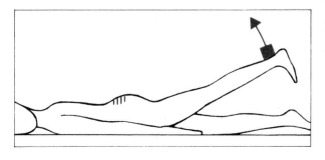

untreated pain lasts 12–14 months): Epidural injection; check no diabetes; bed rest; painkillers; support corset.
(e) Night pain (burning leg pain severe enough to wake at night—not just pain when turning over in bed): Rest; painkillers; epidural injection; support corset.
(f) Shooting pain (down leg): Epidural injection; manipulation; **not** traction. NB If treatment unsuccessful, surgery may be required.

Non-mechanical problems
MUSCLE CRAMP OR SPASM
Cause: Cramp/spasm usually accompanying mechanical problem.

Treatment: *Self*—Rest. Painkillers. Hot-water bottle.
Medical—Treat mechanical problem. Massage. Ultrasound.

LIGAMENT STRAINS IN BACK (COCKTAIL PARTY BACK)
Diagnosis: Stiff and sore first thing in morning but

Living and training with back problems

BACK STRAIN POSITION
Get in the habit of always maintaining the correct back strain position as follows:

LOW BACK STRAIN
Always maintain correct back strain position. Bend from the knees. Avoid reaching for an object from far away. Test its weight by using little lifts until a full one can be made.

HIGH BACK STRAIN
Always maintain correct back strain position. Avoid lifting and twisting to the side, as in picking up and putting down children into cots.

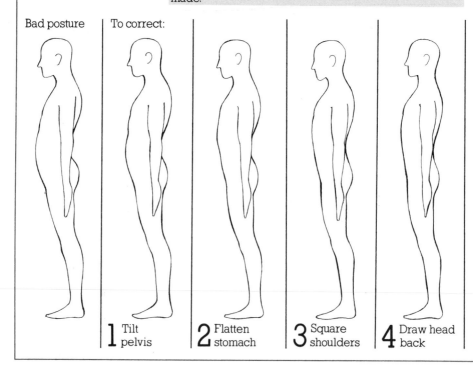

Bad posture　　To correct:

1 Tilt pelvis

2 Flatten stomach

3 Square shoulders

4 Draw head back

eases with movement until you do too much. Sitting or standing for long periods produces dull backache relieved by shifting and moving around. All back movements have full range but *all* (symmetrical) may hurt. Straight leg raise pain-free, though may feel stiff.
Cause: May follow mechanical problems but

also due to bad posture, especially in pregnancy and before menstrual period.
Treatment: *Self*—Maintain back strain position; **do not slouch**, especially when resting. This is a safe back, so sports may be played; back will be trouble-free during exercise but aches and feels weak afterwards.

May need to squat down. Take aspirin rather than non-aspirin painkiller. *Medical*—Anti-inflammatory drugs. Ultrasound. Sugar injections into ligaments to strengthen them.

DISEASE AND CANCER
Any doubts or failure to progress, consult doctor.
See: Rugby (chapter 5).

TIPS FOR GETTING BACK TO NORMAL (for mechanical problems)
1 **Use** back strain position all the time, day in, day out; especially carrying, leaning or bending over.
2 **Stand** with one foot supported 6–8 in off ground.
3 **Sit** with bottom as far back in chair (preferably straight-backed) as possible. Knees should be same height as or lower than hips. Don't sit in low chairs or on low steps as getting up is difficult.
4 **Stand up** by moving bottom to front part of chair, keeping back strain position. Turn sideways and draw both feet (one behind the other) under knees, then stand up in back strain position. Push with hands if possible for more support; choose chairs with arms.
5 **Sleep** on firm mattress or with board underneath mattress. Lie in any position that is

comfortable. With **sciatica** down front of leg and shin, try putting pillow underneath knees when lying on back or underneath hips when lying on front.
6 **Get up** from lying position by turning onto side, bending knees, and sliding feet off bed onto floor. *Then* stand up as in 4.

TRAINING WITH BACK PROBLEMS
Use: Counterbalanced weight machines that support the back sitting or lying down—much better than free weights. Best allow back to be supported whether sitting or lying down.
Avoid:
1 Heavy weights that cannot be lifted easily. Use lighter weights instead, increasing repetitions.
2 Working too fast. Always maintain back strain position.
3 Squats with weights.
4 Step-ups.
5 Lifting weights from floor.

6 Any weight-training that does not keep body supported lying down or that moves it away from vertical position.
7 Doing anything that hurts.

GENERAL FITNESS
Do:
1 Bicycle, but remember to sit upright. If you have drop handlebars, reverse them.
2 Swim, but don't dive or climb out of pool. Use steps. Find most comfortable stroke, probably back crawl.
3 Patter, then skipping routine (pp 101–2).
4 (Only when above can be done with no pain) follow Achilles top ladder.

EXERCISES
Warning: Do not try to work *through* pain. Apply power just until discomfort starts, hold, but go no further.
Calves:
'Heels': Stand on balls of feet on edge of step, facing upstairs. Dropping heels as low as possible, rise to tiptoe and then lower heels slowly.

Quadriceps:

1 Bicycle: Use high resistance with slow pedal rate.
2 Wall exercise: Standing with back straight against wall, slide down so thighs are at about 100° angle to floor, hold 10 sec, rest 10 sec, for 3 min. Do not go lower than 90° angle.
3 Sit in chair with back supported, put carrier bag or basket over foot with bags of sugar inside to make up weight, slowly lift up so leg is straight, counting 5 sec, then lower leg, again taking 5 sec. Repeat 8–10 times.
4 Use quadriceps machine if available.

Hamstrings:

1 Standing, hook heel under chair, pull towards bottom (put weight—another person—on chair).
2 Lie on side on floor, hook heel under lower leg of furniture. Prevent furniture moving by pushing with other leg. Pull heel towards bottom. Alter angle of knee when starting exercise, from nearly straight to fully bent. Hold 10 sec as hard as possible, relax 10 sec, for 2–3 min.
3 Use hamstring training machine if available.

Buttocks:

Sit on floor with legs straight out. 'Walk' forwards on your bottom, then backwards for 2 min.

Stomach muscles:

NB Do not do these exercises if they cause pain.

1 Lie on side on floor, legs straight out, raise top leg, hold 10 sec, relax 10 sec, for 2–3 min.
2 Stand in between two sturdy chairs or two bars. Put forearms on chairbacks/bars and lift body, so legs swing free. Straighten legs, swing them up to hip level (i.e. horizontal) and down again. Repeat as often as comfortable.
3 Sit-ups: Ensure back strain position, lying on back on floor. Make sure small of back is on floor. Lift shoulders, bring upper body into sitting position. Use slow rhythm. Repeat as often as comfortable.
4 Leg raise: Ensure back strain position, lying on back on floor. Make sure small of back is on floor. Lift straight legs, hold 10 sec, then lower. Rest 10 sec. Repeat as often as comfortable.

Back muscles:

Swallows: Lie on stomach on floor, hands behind head, raise shoulders from floor. If able, also raise feet off floor at same time. Hold 10 sec, relax 10 sec, for 2–3 min.
Also: Use back extension machine in gymnasium.

Shoulders:

1 Lie on back on floor, hold book (or weights) in each hand. With arms outstretched (90° angle to chest), raise both arms so books touch over chest.
2 Pull-ups: Hold onto bar or tree branch above head. Pull body up to touch bar with chin only as far as possible, using both overhand and underhand grip to exercise different muscles. Repeat as often as comfortable.
3 Dips: Stand in between bars or chairbacks. Support body weight on hands on bars/chairs. Drop elbows to 90° angle, then raise to straight arms. Repeat as often as comfortable.
4 Press-ups: Lie face down on floor, hands on floor by shoulders. Keep body straight, maintaining back strain position, push shoulders up to arms' length. Drop elbows to right angles, then push straight again. Repeat as often as comfortable.

Hip and pelvis

A strong joint with a wide range of movements. Unfortunately, stretching to maintain this movement is often ignored: compare the movement of an average runner with that of a dancer, gymnast or karate exponent. This is the area where the forces of the two legs are 'hinged' together, so proper muscle build-up is particularly important.

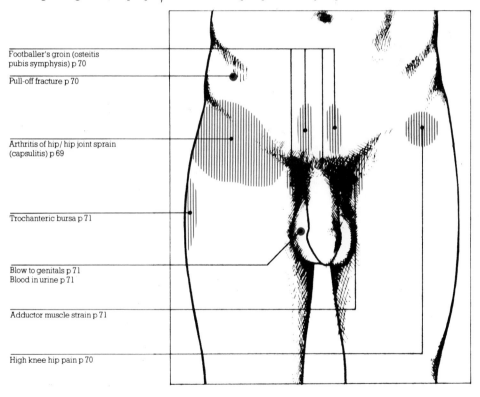

Footballer's groin (osteitis pubis symphysis) p 70

Pull-off fracture p 70

Arthritis of hip/ hip joint sprain (capsulitis) p 69

Trochanteric bursa p 71

Blow to genitals p 71
Blood in urine p 71

Adductor muscle strain p 71

High knee hip pain p 70

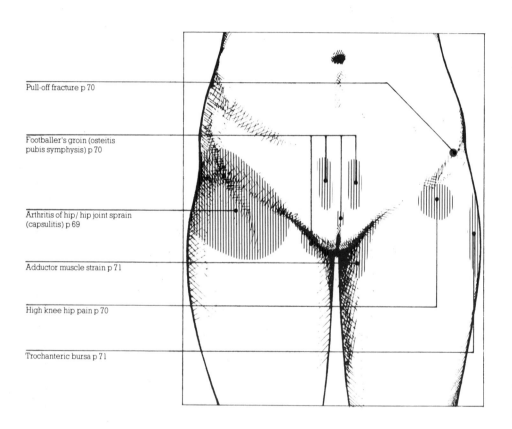

Pull-off fracture p 70

Footballer's groin (osteitis
pubis symphysis) p 70

Arthritis of hip/ hip joint sprain
(capsulitis) p 69

Adductor muscle strain p 71

High knee hip pain p 70

Trochanteric bursa p 71

ARTHRITIS OF HIP/HIP JOINT SPRAIN (CAPSULITIS)

Diagnosis: Lie on back so that leg can be moved as shown in diagrams. Small movements may not hurt but all will be painful at final or extended range. Pain may be felt in knee.

Cause: Wear and tear on joint or hip sprain; latter takes days or 2–3 weeks to get better but arthritis persists after sprain healed. Usually occurs late thirties onwards, but sometimes at very early age.

Treatment: *Self*—Always rest and seek medical help for children. Aspirin. Warm baths. Rest.
Medical—Rest. Anti-inflammatory drugs. Shortwave diathermy. Cortisone injection. Surgery: replacement hip.

Training: Warm bath *before* training may help. Normal general fitness routine; pattering, rowing, bike, but not breaststroke in swimming. Do not overstretch joint in any direction, e.g. keep stride length short. Pattering footwork essential for twisting sports. May signal end of sports involving running or twisting.

See: Golf (chapter 5).

Diagnosis

HIGH KNEE HIP PAIN (PSOAS BURSA)

Diagnosis: Lie on back, leg raised and bent as in diagram. Block movement towards body; pain confirmed at hip joint.

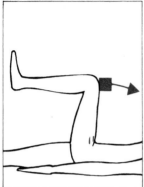

Cause: Overuse makes bursa (or grease bag) under muscle that bends hip sore. Example: sudden increase in sprint training, hill-running, running or speed skating (with upper body leaning forward). Not muscle tear or strain.
Treatment: *Self*—Rest. Stretching exercise 8.
Medical—Ultrasound. Cortisone injection.
Training: Normal general fitness routine, but avoid sprints, hill-running, squat thrusts.
See: Hockey (field), Skating (chapter 5).

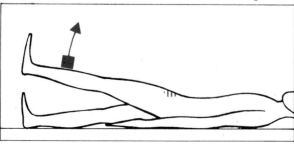

PULL-OFF FRACTURE

Diagnosis: Area hurts to touch; may show bruise or puffy swelling. Lie on back and block upward movement of leg as in diagram at foot of page; pain confirmed at hip joint.
Cause: Muscle pulls away from bone due to very sudden contraction. Usually occurs in teenagers, especially in kicking sports.
Treatment: *Self*—Rest 6–8 weeks.
Medical—Rest 6–8 weeks.
Training: *Fitness*—Hamstring ladders; low gears on bike.
Strength—Heels (see p 112, step 6), upper body work; quads ladder.
Stretch—All stretching exercises but stop at onset of pain with exercises 8, 10, 12.
See: Badminton (chapter 5).

FOOTBALLER'S GROIN (OSTEITIS PUBIS SYMPHYSIS)

Diagnosis: 1 As for Adductor muscle strain, but may produce low stomach pain later.
2 Hurts in middle of pubis.
3 Turning, even turning over in bed, may be painful in low stomach and groin.
4 Sit-ups may hurt.
5 Kicking, sprinting may hurt.
6 Lie on back. Block movement of leg towards body as shown in diagram. Pain confirmed in groin.

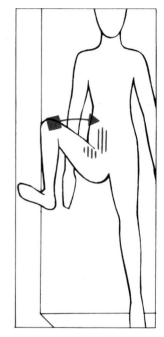

Cause: Ligament joining pelvic bones in front becomes loose. May appear in pregnancy or after giving birth. Thought to be due to overloading one leg more than other as in repeated kicking, high hurdles, or hard sidestep and backing off in front of opponents whilst twisting from side to side (as midfielders in soccer).
Treatment: *Self*—Treat as pull-off fracture, takes months to heal. Rest; patience. Exercise too soon

will reflare. Start stretching again with exercises 4, 9, 10, 12.
Medical—Rest. Treat accompanying adductor muscle. X-ray or scan to help diagnose.
Training: Achilles ladders, taken slowly, then knee ladder.
See: Basketball, Soccer, Hockey (field), Rugby (chapter 5).

ADDUCTOR MUSCLE STRAIN

Diagnosis: 1 Lying down, block leg movement inwards at knee as shown. Pain confirmed in groin. 2 May be tender over bone in groin or just off/on tendon.

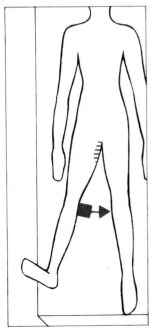

Check for Footballer's groin immediately.
Cause: Adductors pull thighs and knees together, so strain may occur when sidestepping or skipping sideways. Sprinting acceleration, with knees turned in and feet out, may cause strain; also hill-running, when knees and feet are turned out to get shorter stride going uphill, particularly when tired and in mud.
Treatment: *Self*—Rest. ICE. Cross-frictional massage. Stretching exercises 4, 9, 10, 12; if no improvement, see Footballer's groin.
Medical—Ultrasound. Frictional massage. Cortisone injection.
Training: Achilles ladders, then knee ladders.
See: Track and field athletics, Fencing, Badminton, Football (Rugby and American) (chapter 5).

TROCHANTERIC BURSA

Diagnosis: Hurts to press outside of bony point of hip. Movements for arthritis diagnosis do not hurt. Lie on side on floor, painful hip on top, raise and block

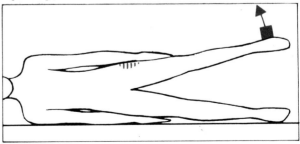

straight leg sideways; pain confirmed.
Cause: Direct blow (squash player slamming into wall) or severe exertion (running extra 5 miles one day) irritates bursa or grease bag; extra fluid inflames area and any movement maintains inflammation.
Treatment: *Self*—Rest. ICE. Aspirin. Avoid sitting with legs crossed at knees; avoid disco-type dancing.
Medical—Ultrasound. Cortisone injection.
Training: Continue as usual, unless painful.

BLOW TO GENITALS

Treatment: *Self*—
Painkillers (men: elevate by wearing support). If blood appears in urine, seek medical advice at once.
See: Waterskiing (chapter 5).

BLOOD IN URINE

Seek medical advice. (May not be serious if it follows exercise.)

Upper leg

The hamstring is at risk in sports where players stop and start suddenly, especially when sprinting. It crosses both knees and hip joints, and at times one end of the muscle is tightening whilst the other is relaxing—think of the whiplash effect going through the muscle at that moment! That is why it is important to build up this coordination as part of the treatment before testing an injured leg in competition.

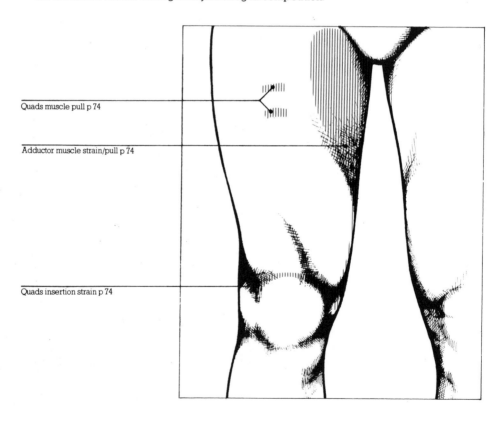

Quads muscle pull p 74

Adductor muscle strain/pull p 74

Quads insertion strain p 74

Trochanteric bursa p 74

Hamstring strains/pulls p 74

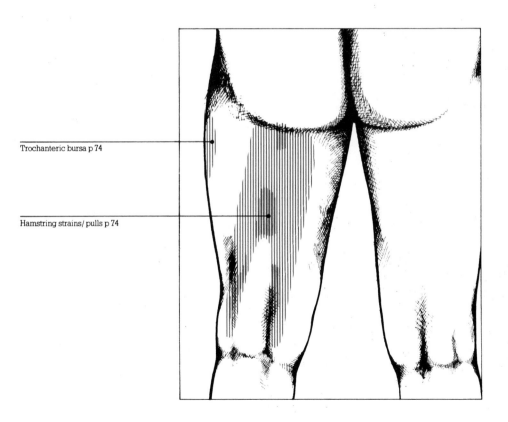

QUADS INSERTION STRAIN

Diagnosis: Pain just above and on top of edge of kneecap. As for Quads muscle pull. See: Quads expansion (p 80).

Cause: Overuse injury, particularly from squats, hill-running, etc. Onset more gradual than quads pull, but same muscle, spreading out over kneecap and its tendons, is involved.

Treatment: *Self*—Rest. ICE. Play usually still possible but injury will persist. Stretching exercises 8, 10. *Medical*—Cross-frictional massage. Ultrasound. Cortisone injection.

Training: Continue as usual, but avoid squats, especially with weights, squat thrusts, step-ups and hill-running. Use quads ladder for strength training.

QUADS MUSCLE PULL

Diagnosis: Front of upper leg hurts to touch. May produce bruise around knee. Soreness when going up stairs, up hills or doing squats. (a) Sitting, block upward movement of leg; pain confirmed. (b) Lying on back, block upward movement of leg at point indicated; pain confirmed.

Cause: Usually central muscle tear, causing damage in 2 areas about 50 mm (2 in) apart. Sometimes muscle tears away from kneecap, producing lump in thigh, especially if kick is blocked.

Treatment: *Self*—ICE. Rest. Stretching exercises 8, 10. Muscle-strapping. *Medical*—Ultrasound. Frictional massage. Surgery, though lump usually left.

Training: Quads ladder.

See: Badminton, Cycling, Gymnastics, Hockey (field), Rugby, Skating, Skiing, Soccer, Squash, Weightlifting (chapter 5).

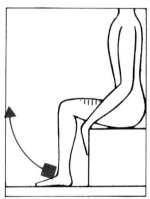

ADDUCTOR MUSCLE STRAIN/PULL

Diagnosis: Hurts to touch. Perhaps bruise over tender spot and/or inside of knee. See: Hip and pelvis, Adductor muscle strain.

Cause: See: Hip and pelvis, Adductor muscle strain.

Treatment: *Self*—See: Hip and pelvis. Also strap for training. Stretching exercises 4, 9 mainly; also 10, 12. *Medical*—Ultrasound. Frictional massage.

Training: Muscle ladder to stage 5; combine with Achilles ladder to stage 8; then knee ladder to stage 5; then Achilles ladder stages 9–12.

See: Badminton, Soccer (chapter 5).

Upper leg/Back

TROCHANTERIC BURSA

See under: Hip and pelvis.

HAMSTRING STRAINS/PULLS

Diagnosis: 1 Tender to touch; tenderness may seem to move around 2–3 different areas during healing.
2 May show bruise over tender area and/or behind knee.
3 Leaning backwards and running hands down either side does not hurt. Check: Low back pain, Sciatica, pp 64–5.
4 Bending to touch toes hurts tender area.
5 (a) Lying on front, block

leg movements as shown;
pain down back of thigh.
(b) Standing in position
shown, bend down towards
leg; pain down back of
thigh.

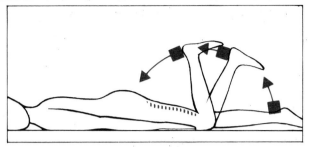

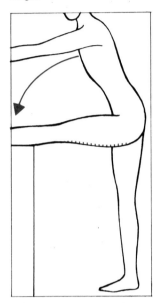

Cause: Movement of hip
and knee out of natural
phase so muscle tears,
especially if hamstring taut
with no reserve elasticity.
Can result from insufficient
warming-up; common in
explosive events involving
sprinting.

Treatment: *Self*—ICE. Rest.
Patience, as will recur if not
fully healed.

Medical—Deep friction
and effluages, massages.
Ultrasound.

Training: Muscle ladder
stages 1–6, combined with
hamstring ladders. Bottom
ladder provides fitness, top
ladder muscle reeducation
which gradually becomes
sprint-type fitness.

Knee

The most injury-prone of all the joints. Severe damage may occur in flat-out competition but most problems are caused in training, where the knee is overused and abused in unbalanced and ill-thought-out sessions.

The anatomy of the knee may also be at fault, and this may be compensated for by altering the balance of the foot. Many training schedules combine strength, endurance and stamina, but these can be broken down into component parts if overuse injuries occur. For example, road race cyclists consistently come into the top fitness group; so why not spend two days of your week on a bicycle to give your knees a rest? You won't be less fit, that's for sure.

Warning: This section should help you *understand* your injury and train with it once it has been diagnosed. Do not try to self-diagnose. This is a diagnostic minefield even for doctors, so see an expert when you suffer knee pain.

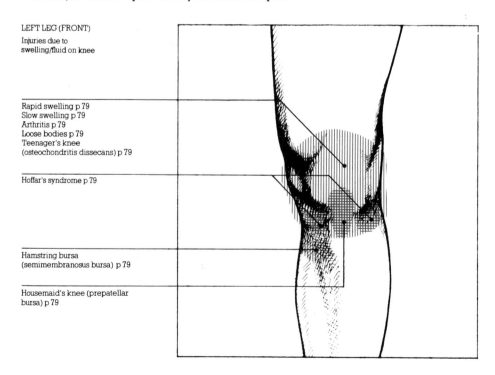

LEFT LEG (FRONT)

Injuries due to
swelling/fluid on knee

Rapid swelling p 79
Slow swelling p 79
Arthritis p 79
Loose bodies p 79
Teenager's knee
(osteochondritis dissecans) p 79

Hoffar's syndrome p 79

Hamstring bursa
(semimembranosus bursa) p 79

Housemaid's knee (prepatellar
bursa) p 79

LEFT LEG (FRONT)

Injuries due to loading thigh
muscle mechanism
(quadriceps)

Quads expansion/insertion p 80

Kneecap soreness
(chondromalacia patellae) p 80

Trapped knee lining
(synovium) p 80

Lower kneecap pain (lower
patella pole) p 80

Jumper's knee (patella
tendinitis) p 80

Osgood Schlatter's disease p 80

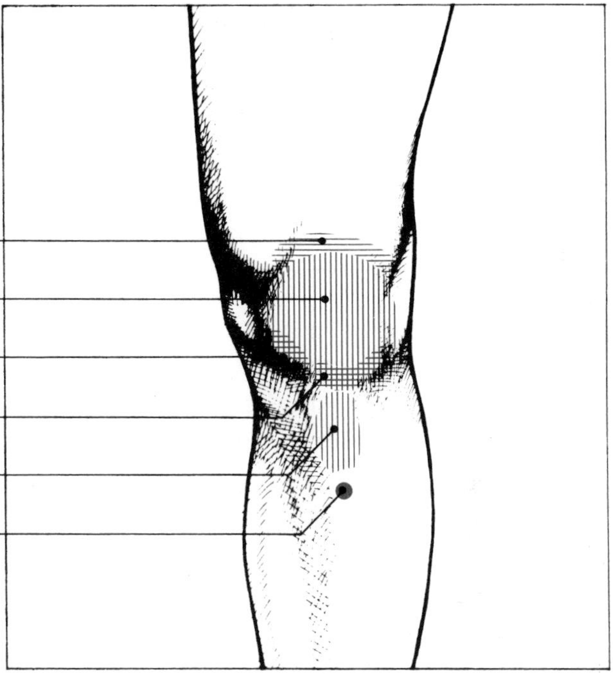

LEFT LEG (OUTSIDE)

Fascia lata strain p 83

Ileotibial tract pain p 83

Lateral ligament strain p 83

Lateral cartilage strain p 82
Lateral cartilage ligament strain p 82

Nerve irritation p 83

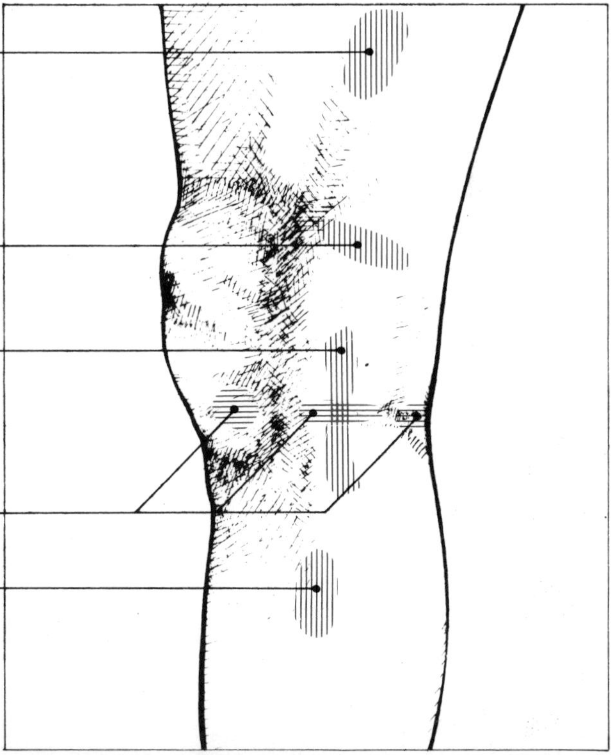

LEFT LEG (INSIDE)

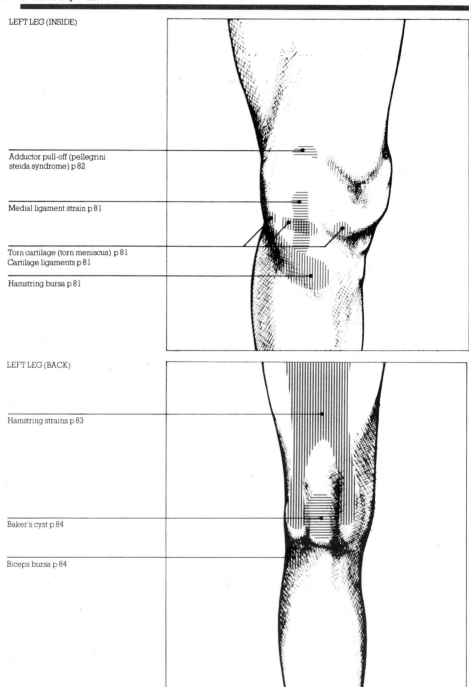

Adductor pull-off (pellegrini steida syndrome) p 82

Medial ligament strain p 81

Torn cartilage (torn meniscus) p 81
Cartilage ligaments p 81

Hamstring bursa p 81

LEFT LEG (BACK)

Hamstring strains p 83

Baker's cyst p 84

Biceps bursa p 84

Swelling/Fluid on knee

HOUSEMAID'S KNEE (PREPATELLAR BURSA)

Diagnosis: May or may not be tender. Fluid under skin but outside knee joint.
Cause: Too much kneeling; direct blow over kneecap.
Treatment: *Self*—Avoid kneeling. Rest. ICE—maintain compression until advised otherwise. Aspirin. *Medical*—Drain off fluid. Cortisone injection. Anti-inflammatory drugs.
Training: Normal general fitness routine.
See: Canoeing, Shooting (chapter 5).

HOFFAR'S SYNDROME

Diagnosis: Hollows either side of knee joint appear swollen (this is fat, not fluid); tender to press.
Cause: Overuse, usually in long-distance runners, especially at end of run, or joggers increasing mileage too suddenly. Hill-running, particularly downhill, can bring it on.
Treatment: *Self*—Rest. ICE. Aspirin. Check shoes have thick, absorbent soles. *Medical*—Ultrasound. Cortisone injection.
Training: Reduce mileage. Run on grass if possible. Avoid downhill runs.

HAMSTRING BURSA (SEMIMEMBRANOSUS BURSA)

Diagnosis: Inside and lower part of knee tender to touch.
Cause: Overuse of hamstrings.
Treatment: *Self*—Rest. ICE. Aspirin. *Medical*—Ultrasound. Frictional massage. Cortisone injection.
Training: Continue as usual, but avoid rapid knee bends as in cycling or sprinting, especially if knees splay outwards.

LOOSE BODIES

Diagnosis: Knee may lock. May be swelling.
Cause: Loose fragments of cartilage or bone within knee.
Treatment: *Self*—Rest. ICE. Aspirin. *Medical*—Manipulate clear. X-ray. Arthroscope. Surgery.
Training: Rest. Knee ladder under medical supervision.

TEENAGER'S KNEE (OSTEOCHONDRITIS DISSECANS)

Diagnosis: On X-ray only.
Cause: Small piece of bone and cartilage separates and can form loose body in knee joint. More common in boys.
Treatment: *Self*—Rest. ICE. Aspirin. *Medical*—Surgery.
Training: Rest. Knee ladder under medical supervision.

ARTHRITIS

Diagnosis: Knee may be painful at rest, worse with movement. Fully straightening and fully bending hurt. May cause swelling.
Cause: As cartilage wears down, kneebones roughen from grating together. May follow surgical removal of meniscus.
Treatment: *Self*—Rest. Aspirin. Warm bath. *Medical*—Anti-inflammatory drugs. Shortwave diathermy. Cortisone injection. Surgery.
Training: Do not overexercise joint; space out training with rest intervals. May signal end of really active sports, games.

RAPID SWELLING (WITHIN 2–4 HR)

Diagnosis: Swelling occurs within 2–4 hr.
Cause: Sudden strain. Check for serious damage as ligament may have torn with blood in joint.
Treatment: *Self*—Rest. ICE; maintain compression until advised otherwise. Seek medical advice within 2–4 days—at latest within 14 days. Aspirin. *Medical*—Drain fluid. Cortisone injection. Arthroscope. Arthrogram. Physiotherapy. Surgery.
Training: Heels. Quads ladder. Sit-ups. Upper body strength. Knee ladder.
See: Badminton (chapter 5).

SLOW SWELLING (FROM 6–24 HR)

Diagnosis: Swelling occurs from 6–24 hr.
Cause: Varied—may be sprained or sprung, or as serious as torn cartilage.
Treatment: *Self*—Rest. ICE; maintain ice and compression over 7–14 days, may settle by itself. Aspirin.

Medical—As for Rapid swelling.
Training: See Rapid swelling.

Injuries due to loading thigh muscle mechanism

QUADS EXPANSION/INSERTION

Diagnosis: Pain at top of kneecap.
Cause: Overload of quads muscles.
Treatment: *Self*—Rest. ICE. Frictional massage.
Medical—Deep friction massage. Ultrasound. Cortisone injection. Orthotics.
Training: Quads ladder. Avoid strenuous bent knees exercise, i.e. climbing hills, squats, step-ups, squat thrusts, weights.
See: Badminton, Cycling, Gymnastics, Hockey (field), Rugby, Skating, Skiing, Squash, Weightlifting (chapter 5).

KNEECAP SORENESS (CHONDROMALACIA PATELLAE)

Diagnosis: Pain on either or both sides of kneecap. Difficult to bend knee. More common in women.
Cause: Inflammation at back of kneecap. Possibly due to faulty alignment of kneecap in groove of thighbone; also overloading quadriceps muscles (weights,

hill-runnning, etc.).
Treatment: *Self*—Rest. Lie on floor with light (2 kg) weight on ankle of sore leg, put cushion under knee and flex leg from straight to 20° bend *only*; build up weight gradually but *not* degree of bend.
Medical—Shortwave diathermy. Differential faradism. Surgery.
Training: Quads ladder. Avoid strenuous bent knee exercise, i.e. hills, squats, step-ups, squat thrusts, weights (bike work may be painful).
See: Badminton, Cycling, Gymnastics, Hockey (field), Rowing, Rugby, Skating, Skiing, Squash, Weightlifting (chapter 5).

LOWER KNEECAP PAIN (LOWER PATELLA POLE)

Diagnosis: Lower end of kneecap tender to touch.
Cause: Overload, often by athletes who land or take off on one leg; also possible both legs.
Treatment: *Self*—Deep friction massage.
Medical—Deep friction massage. Ultrasound. Cortisone injection.
Training: Quads ladder. Avoid strenuous bent knee exercise, i.e. hills, squats, step-ups, squat thrusts, weights.
See: Badminton, Cricket, Cycling, Gymnastics, Hockey (field), Rugby, Skating, Skiing, Squash, Swimming, Weightlifting (chapter 5).

TRAPPED KNEE LINING (SYNOVIUM)

Diagnosis: Pain either side of kneecap. Some movements painfree. Hurts to run, especially hill-running.
Cause: Kneecap rubbing against thighbone.
Treatment: *Self*—Rest.
Medical—Cortisone injection. Frictional massage. Surgery.
Training: Quads ladder. Avoid strenuous bent knee exercise, i.e. hills, squats, step-ups, squat thrusts, weights. Work on heels, patter routine, hamstring ladder.

JUMPER'S KNEE (PATELLA TENDINITIS)

Diagnosis: Thick tendon below kneecap tender to touch.
Cause: Overuse in jumping sports. Damaged tendon.
Treatment: *Self*—Rest. ICE. Cross-frictional massage.
Medical—Rest. Ultrasound. Cross-frictional massage. Surgery.
Training: Quads ladder. Avoid strenuous bent knee exercise, i.e. hills, squats, step-ups, squat thrusts, weights.
See: Badminton, Squash (chapter 5).

OSGOOD SCHLATTER'S DISEASE

Diagnosis: *Not* disease but inflammation. Swelling and tenderness over knob below kneecap. Occurs only in growing children.
Cause: Overuse; straining growing area where tendon attaches. Does not

occur when growth ceases.
Treatment: *Self*—Rest 4–12
weeks.
Medical—Rest
(ultrasound). Surgery.
Training: Continue as usual,
unless produces pain.
Quads ladder. Avoid
strenuous bent knee
exercise, i.e. hills, squats,
step-ups, squat thrusts,
weights, until over 16 years
old approx.
See: Badminton, Diving,
Squash, Track and field
athletics, Weightlifting.

Pain on inside of knee

HAMSTRING BURSA
See p 79.

TORN CARTILAGE (TORN MENISCUS)
Medial cartilage is on
inside of knee, Lateral
cartilage on outside.
Diagnosis: Gap between
kneebones tender to press.
Knee may be swollen. May
stick, lock or click. Twisting
and squatting may hurt.
Cause: Forceful twisting
tears or splits cartilage, the
'shock absorber' in knee.
Treatment: *Self*—Rest. ICE.
Avoid twisting movements.
Medical—Manipulate if
locked. Arthrogram.
Arthroscopy. Surgery.
Training: Quads ladder.
Essential to maintain quads
strength before and after
operation. Rowing may be
trouble-free.

CARTILAGE LIGAMENTS
Diagnosis: Leg may not

lock, but will 'catch' with
pain on certain knee
movements. No swelling
unless accompanied by
other damage (i.e. torn
cartilage). Tender to
pressure over joint line or
in hollows either side of
knee, below kneecap.
Cause: Ligaments are
trapped between upper
and lower legbone. Can be
caused by running on
camber or hump of road
where, effectively, one leg
is 'longer' than the other;
also running with lower
legs 'flailing' or
'windmilling' sideways
(see diagram); also in

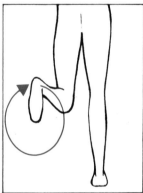

hill-running, when tired
legs mean lower knee lift
and feet splayed sideways;
also sitting cross-legged, or
feet tucked underneath
chair or bottom.
Treatment: *Self*—Rest.
Massage over tender spot.
Avoid hill-running, uneven
surfaces. Mount slopes
zigzag fashion using short
strides, foot planted
directly below knee.
Medical—Frictional
massage. Ultrasound.
Cortisone injection.

Training: Continue as usual
unless painful, but cut down
mileage, using several
short circuits rather than
one long one so you can
return home if pain
reoccurs; ensure knee lift is
high, to diminish rotation of
lower leg. Avoid hills and
rough ground until better.
As kneeling or squatting
may hurt, drop to one knee
if you have to. Knee ladder
for ball games.
See: Rugby, Sailing, Skiing,
Soccer, Swimming (chapter
5).

MEDIAL LIGAMENT STRAIN
Diagnosis: Pressing lower
leg out sideways hurts.
Tender to touch on inside of
knee over joint line and just
on either side over
thighbone and on
shinbone. Lying on back,

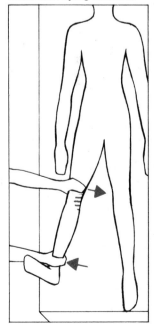

legs apart as shown, leg is moved both out and in; pain confirmed on inside of knee.

Cause: Severe wrenching of knee joint as lower leg goes outwards and sideways. May be severe enough to tear part or all of ligaments.

Treatment: *Self*—ICE, especially compression, using support strapping or knee support reaching 15 cm (6 in) above and below knee; too short a support is useless. Wear all day, every day, until knee ladder started, then use in training and for first 6 weeks of competition. IMPORTANT: This treatment is sufficient if ligament not ruptured. If in doubt, see doctor within 10 days.

Medical—Rest. Plaster cast. Strapping. Frictional massage. Ultrasound. Surgery.

Training: As this ligament is vital to knee stability it must *not* be put at risk. Can take 3–4 months to heal. Continue upper body work. Use quads ladders *without* pattering. Knee ladder. All exercise to be done with knee support in place, also first 6 weeks of competition.

See: Skiing (chapter 5).

ADDUCTOR PULL-OFF (PELLEGRINI STEIDA SYNDROME)

Diagnosis: Highest knob of bone on inside of knee painful to pressure. Squeezing fist between knees causes pain over tender area. Lying on back, block inward movement of raised leg as shown; pain confirmed.

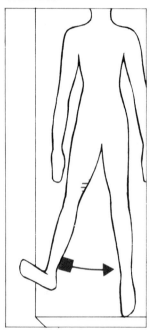

Cause: Muscle or ligament on inside of thigh is pulled off when knee is wrenched; complicated by build-up of calcium and bone.

Treatment: *Self*—ICE for 24 hr. Thorough rest required as exercise produces complication of new bone build-up; take medical advice before resuming even light exercise.

Medical—Rest. Surgery.

Training: Muscle ladder. Hamstring ladder to step 9, then knee ladder.

See: Ball games and racquet sports (chapter 5).

Pain on outside of knee

Most of these injuries are due to overuse strains but they are more frequent with bow legs, pigeon toes, running markedly on the outside of the foot or 'flailing' or 'windmilling' the lower leg.

LATERAL CARTILAGE STRAIN

See Torn cartilage and Cartilage ligaments (p 81). Lump felt on outside of knee joint comes and goes with knee movements. Caused by swelling in cartilage; if no trouble leave alone, if bothersome may need surgery.

LATERAL CARTILAGE LIGAMENT STRAIN

Diagnosis: Does not lock knee; no swelling unless complicated by other knee problems. Twisting knee, full squat position and kneeling may hurt. Painful over gap between bones and/or in hollow on front of knee.

Cause: Severe twist or continual pressure (even sitting cross-legged or with legs tucked under).

Treatment: *Self*—Rest. ICE. Massage. Orthotics.

Medical—Rest. Cross-frictional massage. Ultrasound. Orthotics.

Training: Continue as usual, but if too painful keep fit with rowing or crawl swimming. Avoid deep knee bends. Burpees (gymnastics). Avoid running on camber or hump of road, especially with painful knee higher. 'Flailing' or 'windmilling' lower leg should be avoided, also stopping suddenly using outside of foot. When running, concentrate on lifting knee, shorter stride and smooth heel/toe action as foot lands. Avoid hill-running. Zigzag up slopes if you have to.

See: Soccer, Track and field athletics (pole vault) (chapter 5).

ILEOTIBIAL TRACT PAIN

Diagnosis: When hand follows groove in outside of thigh, leg feels tender at bony knob on outside of knee. Hurts as knee bends ileotibial tract from straight through 20–30°.

Cause: Overuse in runners with awkward running styles (see introduction).

Treatment: *Self*—ICE. Frictional massage. Rest 4–5 days. Orthotics. *Medical*—Massage. Ultrasound. Cortisone injection. Orthotics. Surgery.

Training: Alter 'one-pace' running pattern. Avoid running on cambered (humped) road where painful knee is lower.

FASCIA LATA STRAIN

Diagnosis: Pain in hollow or groove running down lower side of thigh to knee.

Cause: Overuse in runners with awkward running styles.

Treatment: *Self*—Rest. ICE. Orthotics. *Medical*—Rest. Ultrasound. Orthotics.

Training: Avoid running downhill at speed and on camber or hump of road.

LATERAL LIGAMENT STRAIN

Diagnosis: Painful over gap between bones and over bones themselves. Hurts to force legs into 'bow leg' position.

Cause: Wrenching knee sprains or tears ligament that holds knee in place.

Treatment: *Self*—Rest. ICE. Strapping or elastic support reaching 15 cm (6 in) above and below knee; too short a support is useless. Wear all day, every day, until knee ladder started, then use for exercise and for first 6 weeks of competition. Orthotics. IMPORTANT: This treatment is sufficient if ligament not ruptured. If in doubt, see doctor within 10 days. *Medical*—Rest. Plaster cast. Anti-inflammatory drugs. Ultrasound. Cross-frictional massage. Strapping. Orthotics. Surgery.

Training: **No** running. Swim, row, do bike routine, patter routine through to knee ladder under medical direction. Maintain quads ladder. Keep strapping throughout and for 6–8 weeks once back in action.

UNSTABLE KNEE (CRUCIATE LIGAMENT TEARS)

Diagnosis: Only by doctor. (Check Medial ligament strain, p 81, and Lateral ligament strain.)

Cause: Wrenched knee.

Treatment: *Self*—Support or strapping. *Medical*—Physiotherapy. Surgery. Braced knee support.

Training: Under medical supervision. Quads ladder. As most contact sports do not allow use of knee-brace, you may have to change to new sport.

See: Badminton (chapter 5).

NERVE IRRITATION

Diagnosis: Pain and/or numbness on outside of lower leg. Reproduced by pressing hollow just below lowest bony knob on outside of leg below knee.

Cause: Damage, irritation to nerve after direct blow or awkward fall—even sitting with knees crossed!

Treatment: *Self*—Painkillers. Will get better in 3 weeks or so. Avoid sitting cross-legged. *Medical*—Painkillers. Cortisone injection. Surgery.

Training: Continue as usual.

Pain on back of knee

HAMSTRING STRAINS

See under: Upper leg/Back. May show up as bruises around knee. Will heal faster than same-sized tear that does not produce bruise.

BAKER'S CYST

Diagnosis: Lump in middle of back of knee that gets more tense after exercise. Felt as swelling or tightening.

Cause: Fluid sac pops out 'backwards' in knee. May leak internally causing swelling in calf, ankle.

Treatment: *Self*—Rest. Ignore if possible. *Medical*—Do nothing. Surgery.

Training: Continue as usual.

BICEPS BURSA

Yes, one of the hamstring muscles is also called the biceps!

Diagnosis: Bony point on outside of knee is tender just under tendon or on tendon itself.

Cause: Common in fast leg-action sports with fast high heel lift (i.e. sprinting).

Treatment: *Self*—Rest. ICE. *Medical*—Rest. Ultrasound. Frictional massage. Cortisone injection.

Training: Continue as usual. Avoid repetition sprint sessions until better. Bend running on track may also make this flare up.

Lower leg

Endurance training should be done on soft ground, since road running is jarring and may lead to stress fractures. The Achilles heel has a place in mythology with reason: it causes most problems in this area of the body. Do not rush back to your sport before you have worked right through the Achilles ladder. Why play at 80 per cent fitness for the next year when proper treatment can get you 100 per cent fit?

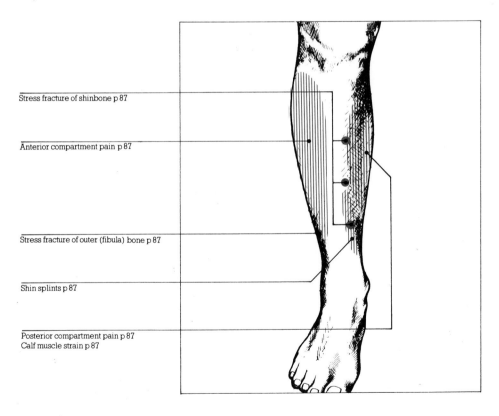

Stress fracture of shinbone p 87

Anterior compartment pain p 87

Stress fracture of outer (fibula) bone p 87

Shin splints p 87

Posterior compartment pain p 87
Calf muscle strain p 87

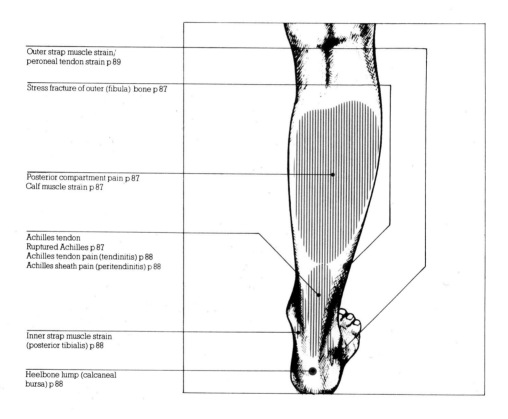

Outer strap muscle strain/
peroneal tendon strain p 89

Stress fracture of outer (fibula) bone p 87

Posterior compartment pain p 87
Calf muscle strain p 87

Achilles tendon
Ruptured Achilles p 87
Achilles tendon pain (tendinitis) p 88
Achilles sheath pain (peritendinitis) p 88

Inner strap muscle strain
(posterior tibialis) p 88

Heelbone lump (calcaneal
bursa) p 88

STRESS FRACTURE OF SHINBONE

Diagnosis: Hurts on starting exercise like running. Settles with rest. Painful to touch over small area (1–2 cm/1 in). Painful to walk. Common third of way *down* from knee and *up* from ankle, but can also occur midway between knee and ankle.

Cause: Overuse, often through running distances on hard surfaces to build up mileage. 'Bounding' style of running more susceptible than shuffling, low-knee lift style.

Treatment: *Self*—Rest from running for 5–6 weeks. Occasionally, strapping from knee to ankle may help.
Medical—Rest. Orthotics.

Training: Avoid *all* running for 5–6 weeks. Maintain other fitness by swimming, rowing, bike routines. After 5 weeks, hamstring ladder. Check shoes well padded, then avoid running on hard surfaces. Try shorter stride pattern and ensure correct foot placement as you run.
See: Track and field athletics, Skating (chapter 5).

STRESS FRACTURE OF OUTER (FIBULA) BONE

Diagnosis: When running or walking, pain occurs approximately one hand's breadth above outside anklebone. Hurts to press.

Cause: Running with weight on outside of foot, common to bowlegs, and landing pigeon-toed on ball of foot.

Treatment: *Self and Medical*—as for Stress fracture of shinbone.
Training: As for Stress fracture of shinbone, but try to correct pigeon-toed gait.

SHIN SPLINTS

Diagnosis: Pain along inner or outer edge of shinbone. Worse after exercise. Area 2–7 cm (1–3 in) tender to pressure.

Cause: Overuse strain, producing tearing and thickening of muscles at join along shinbone. May be accompanied by stress fracture.

Treatment: *Self*—Rest. ICE.
Medical—Rest. ICE. Ultrasound. Surgery.
Training: Achilles ladders. Heels. Build up mileage slowly. Upper body work as usual.

POSTERIOR COMPARTMENT PAIN

Diagnosis: Calf muscle painful after exercise, long exertion.

Cause: Overuse of calf muscle. Leg muscle cannot expand in its tight sheath.

Treatment: *Self*—Rest. ICE, especially ice and elevation. Painkillers.
Medical—ICE. Ultrasound. Surgery to release sheath.
Training: Continue as usual.

ANTERIOR COMPARTMENT PAIN

Diagnosis: Pain in muscles on front and outside of shin after exercise. Tender to press.

Cause: Overuse of muscles that lift forefoot and toes off ground. Muscle cannot expand in its tight sheath.

Treatment: *Self*—Rest. ICE, especially ice and elevation. Painkillers.
Medical—ICE. Ultrasound. Surgery to release sheath.
Training: Continue as usual, but avoid repeat work in hills, rough ground, long 'step-up' sessions.
See: Skiing (chapter 5).

CALF MUSCLE STRAIN

Diagnosis: May feel like sudden kick or blow on calf. Hurts in calf when rising on tiptoe. Tender to press. May bruise.

Cause: Overload tears calf muscle.

Treatment: *Self*—Rest. ICE, especially compression. Takes about 1–5 weeks to heal.
Medical—Ultrasound. Massage.
Training: Upper body work as usual. Achilles ladder. Stretching exercises 1, 2, 9, 10, 11, 12 (especially 1, 2, 12).

Achilles tendon

The tendon that runs from the calf to the heel is strong but does not have much blood supply, so while it does not tire, small tears and damage do not heal easily. With proper treatment, healing takes 4–16 weeks.

RUPTURED ACHILLES

Diagnosis: Sudden sharp pain may feel like kick or blow in leg. Cannot rise on tiptoe on that foot.
Lie on bed face down, feet hanging over end; good

foot has angle of 20–30° to vertical, bad foot hangs straight down at 90°. Squeeze calf with hand; good foot will move outwards, bad foot will not move.

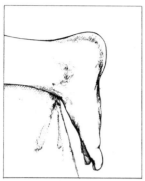

Ruptured Achilles

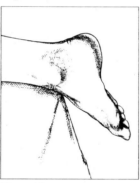

Normal foot

Cause: Tendon cannot take load and snaps. More frequent in older people.
Treatment: *Self*—ICE. Heel raise. See doctor within 3–4 days.
Medical—Heel raise and plaster cast. Surgery.
Training: Supervised by doctor, Achilles ladders.

ACHILLES TENDON PAIN (TENDINITIS)
Diagnosis: Pain in thick

tendon of calf muscle. May develop lump if not allowed to heal properly. May be stiff in morning; hurts to rise on tiptoes; hurts to run.
See also: Ankle, Jumper's/dancer's heel.
Cause: Minor tear of Achilles tendon.
Treatment: *Self*—Rest. ICE. Heel raise. **Do not** return to activities until training ladders completed. Hurrying back too soon will result in large scar and permanent pain.
Medical—Heel raise. Ultrasound. Cross-frictional massage. Stretching. Surgery.
Training: Achilles ladders. Stretching exercises 1, 2, 9, 10, 11, 12 (especially 1, 2, 12).

ACHILLES SHEATH PAIN (PERITENDINITIS)
Diagnosis: Take foot in hand and move forefoot up and down; pain over Achilles.
Cause: Heel tab or so-called 'Achilles protector' on sports shoes may press or jam into Achilles, causing damage. Often accompanies Achilles tendon pain (see above), producing thickening and roughening of Achilles tendon lining.
Treatment: *Self*—Rest. ICE. Massage. Aspirin. Cut off Achilles protector tab on shoes and tape down rough edge.
Medical—Anti-inflammatory drugs. Ultrasound. Deep friction massage. Cortisone

injection. Surgery.
Training: Achilles ladders. Stretching exercises 1, 2, 9, 10, 11, 12 (especially 1, 2, 12).

HEELBONE LUMP (CALCANEAL BURSA)
Diagnosis: Bony knob of heel is tender. Does not hurt to rise barefoot on tiptoe. May be hot, red and puffy.
Cause: Shoe rubbing on skin of heel.
Treatment: *Self*—ICE. Aspirin. Stretch heel of shoe, cover with shiny plaster and soap outside of plaster to allow shoe to slip. Try bigger shoe with two pairs of socks. 'Second skin' type of plastic aid.
Medical—Anti-inflammatory drugs. Ultrasound. Cortisone injection. Surgery.
Training: Continue as usual. If sore to run, train with patter, bike routines with no shoes; swimming routine.

INNER STRAP MUSCLE STRAIN (POSTERIOR TIBIALIS)
Diagnosis: Pain behind and

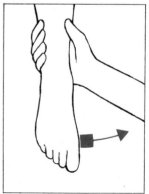

beneath inner anklebone. May also extend down side of foot and underneath arch. Block inward movement of foot as shown; pain confirmed.

Cause: Strain of balancing muscle of foot counteracting flat feet and rolling over inside of foot may strain this tendon and its sheath, especially in long-distance running and overwork on points in ballet.

Treatment: *Self*—ICE. Massage. Arch support. Practise picking up pencil in toes to raise arch of foot. Standing up, concentrate on 'pulling' knees backwards and outwards using muscles only; weight on outside of foot, raising arch. Wear good shoes with strong heel cup and arch support; stirrup strap. See: Ankle, Flat foot pain, Sprained ankle.

Medical—Ultrasound. Cross-frictional massage. Cortisone injection. Arch support. Orthotics.

Training: Rest from running. Bike, swimming, rowing routines. Build up running via Achilles top ladder.

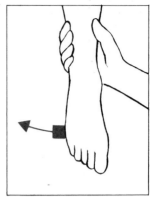

OUTER STRAP MUSCLE STRAIN/PERONEAL TENDON STRAIN

Diagnosis: Pain behind and under outer anklebone. May extend down outside of foot and underneath. Block outward movement of foot as shown; pain confirmed.

Cause: Strain balancing muscles of foot, sometimes following twisted ankle; strain of counteracting pigeon-toed running gait or where weight is heavily on outside of foot. Tendon may even slip over outside anklebone, causing 'flicking' and pain.

Treatment: *Self*—Rest. ICE. Massage tender areas. Aspirin. Stirrup strap (see diagram). Try cutting insole lengthwise and putting outer half in shoe to raise outer edge of foot.

Medical—Anti-inflammatory drugs. Ultrasound. Cross-frictional massage. Cortisone injection. Surgery. Orthotics.

Training: Avoid running until better. Swimming, bike, rowing routines. Build through Achilles top ladder.

See: Squash (chapter 5).

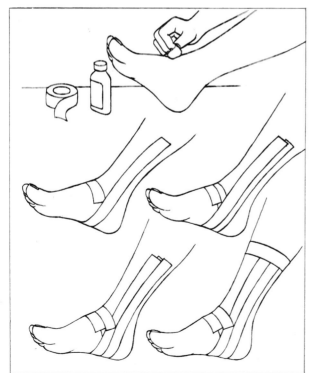

Ankle

The stresses and strains of balancing, checking, turning and running on rough ground are all focused on this area, which is probably second only to the knee in vulnerability to injuries. Until recovery is complete, strapping to support the ligaments is helpful, as are orthotics, which can alter an unstable foot position and help with balance.

Warning: A difficult area to make accurate diagnosis, so consult doctor if any doubts.
NB Also check diagnostic tests for Lower leg, pp 85–9.

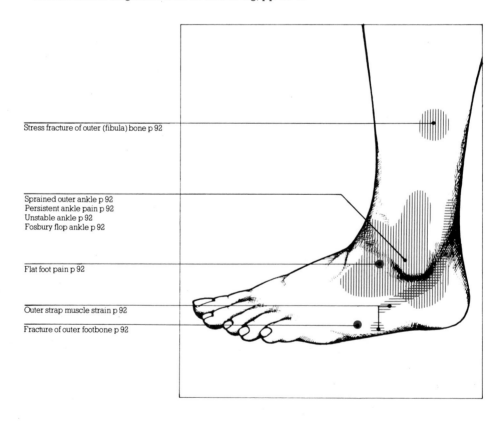

Stress fracture of outer (fibula) bone p 92

Sprained outer ankle p 92
Persistent ankle pain p 92
Unstable ankle p 92
Fosbury flop ankle p 92

Flat foot pain p 92

Outer strap muscle strain p 92

Fracture of outer footbone p 92

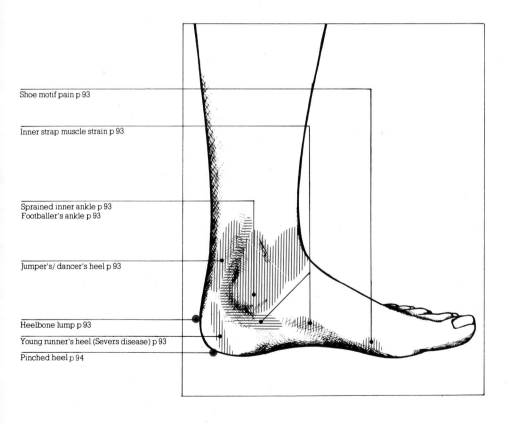

Shoe motif pain p 93

Inner strap muscle strain p 93

Sprained inner ankle p 93
Footballer's ankle p 93

Jumper's/ dancer's heel p 93

Heelbone lump p 93

Young runner's heel (Severs disease) p 93

Pinched heel p 94

SPRAINED OUTER ANKLE

Diagnosis: Some or all of the following apply:
(a) painful at rest;
(b) first few paces excruciating, then eases up whilst walking, but severe pain again on stopping;
(c) red, swollen, bruised to sole of foot, feels warm;
(d) hurts when heelbone is moved inwards or big toe pointed downwards and inwards (see diagrams);
(e) hurts to touch.

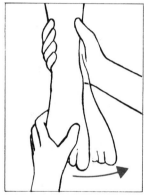

Cause: 'Turning ankle over' onto outside of foot.
Treatment: *Self*—Rest. ICE, especially compression and elevation. Aspirin if severe. Avoid weight on ankle, use crutches 48 hr. Support strapping (see p 89)—maintain at night. Try using cardboard box as cage to lift bedclothes off ankle.
When walking: Maintain strapping; take smaller steps and try to walk heel/toe with foot pointing straight ahead; later, balance along kerb edge and walk along lines in pavement. Practise balance on 'wobble board' (round platform attached to sphere).
Medical—ICE. Ultrasound. Wobble board. Cross-frictional massage.
Training: Continue upper body work. Bike, rowing routines as soon as able. Wobble board. Knee ladder with strapping. Maintain strapping for 6 weeks after resuming competition.

PERSISTENT ANKLE PAIN

Diagnosis: Stiff, painful ankle movements persisting 4–6 weeks after sprained ankle. See diagnosis diagrams for sprained ankle.
Cause: Ligaments heal but mobility of joint not fully restored. Scar tissue stiffens joint.
Treatment: *Self*—Seek medical advice.
Medical—Manipulation. Cortisone injection. Then, as for Sprained outer ankle.
Training: Continue as usual.

UNSTABLE ANKLE

Diagnosis: Only by doctor.
Cause: Wrenched ankle.
Treatment: *Self*—Support or strapping (see p 89).
Medical—Strapping. Plaster casts. Surgery.
Training: Under medical supervision, maintain quads; rowing, bike routines; then, patter routine, Achilles and knee ladders.

FOSBURY FLOP ANKLE

See: Track and field athletics (chapter 5).

OUTER STRAP MUSCLE STRAIN

See under: Lower leg.

FRACTURE OF OUTER FOOTBONE

Seek medical advice.

STRESS FRACTURE OF OUTER (FIBULA) BONE

See under: Lower leg.

FLAT FOOT PAIN

Diagnosis: Pain over front of outside anklebone when pressed and also when foot lifted up and outwards.
Cause: Flat foot rolls over inside, causing strain on inner strap muscle and joints but running forces outside foot up into outer anklebone.
Treatment: *Self*—Arch support, often with wedge under big toe joint. Good shoes strengthened with heel cup and inner support. Try stirrup strap (see p 89), starting on outside of foot, under and up over inside of ankle, correcting rolled-over arch. Pick up pencil in toes and, standing up, draw knees back and

outwards, using muscles only. Practise regularly every day.
Medical—Arch support. Faradism to feet muscles. Orthotics.
Training: Continue as usual, corrective mechanism in place.

SPRAINED INNER ANKLE

Diagnosis: Pain on and below inner anklebone. May have swelling and bruising that will discolour foot. Pain on forcing foot upwards and outwards (see diagrams).
Cause: 'Turning ankle over' onto inside of foot. Not as

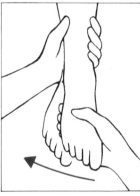

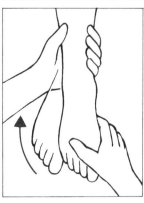

common as outer ankle sprain. Check with doctor, as fracture or unstable rupture may occur.
Treatment: *Self*—See: Sprained outer ankle.
Medical—See: Sprained outer ankle.
Training: See: Sprained outer ankle.
See: Basketball, Handball, Netball, Volleyball (chapter 5).

HEELBONE LUMP
See under: Lower leg.

FOOTBALLER'S ANKLE

Diagnosis: Thickened ankle area that may hurt to touch. May hurt to move or may be painfree.
Cause: Sprain of ankle ligaments, especially inner, from side foot tackle or blocked kick. X-rays reveal small fragments of bone and calcium from repeated direct kicks and sprains.
Treatment: *Self*—ICE. Aspirin. Shin pads with ankle flaps, or felt/foam ankle padding under socks. May require strapping.
Medical—ICE. Anti-inflammatory drugs.
Training: Continue as usual.
See: Basketball, Handball, Football (chapter 5).

SHOE MOTIF PAIN

Diagnosis: Sore area of skin; may even be rubbed raw. Usually hurts on inside of shoe.
Cause: Shoe motif decorations are usually plastic and do not expand with leather of shoe. This

can cause pressure on foot near motif's attachment to sole.
Treatment: *Self*—Slit across motif near attachment to sole of shoe.

INNER STRAP MUSCLE STRAIN
See under: Lower leg.

YOUNG RUNNER'S HEEL (SEVERS DISEASE)

Diagnosis: Not a disease! Hurts as foot strikes ground, sometimes on takeoff for jumping.
Cause: Overuse damages 'growing points' of heelbone.
Treatment: *Self*—Aspirin. Rest.
Medical—Rest.
Training: No running. Swimming, bike, rowing routines. Build into patter routine if no pain, then Achilles top ladder. Maintain quads, heels and upper body strength throughout.

JUMPER'S/DANCER'S HEEL

Diagnosis: Pain on pressure between Achilles tendon and back of anklebones. Hurts on 'full points' or tiptoe. Hurts on takeoff but not landing. Pain confirmed by forcibly jamming heel against back of shinbone, by snapping foot downwards.
Cause: 1 Repeatedly rising on tiptoe (dancer's points). 2 Explosive jumping. 3 Foot blocked as ball is kicked with toes pointing downwards.

4 'Stamping' heel down when finishing movement.
5 Causes 1–4 compress pad of fat between heelbone and shinbone. Sometimes, however, a bone (os trigonum) is present, like a nut between these nutcrackers—result is pain.
Treatment: *Self*—Rest. Aspirin.
Medical—Anti-inflammatory drugs.

Ultrasound. Cortisone injection. Surgical removal of os trigonum bone.
Training: Avoid 'points', jumping (high, long and triple jump) and bounding routines if sore. Exercise probably safe but pain will recur. Maintain heels. Use Achilles ladder.
See: Soccer (chapter 5).

PINCHED HEEL
Diagnosis: Painful skin and soft tissue under back of heel.
Cause: Bruising of skin and pad of fat under heelbone.
Treatment: *Self*—Insert firmer heel cup to shoe and large absorbent heel; or use absorbent rubber heel pads.
Medical—Rest.
Training: Continue as usual if no pain.

Foot and toes

Athlete's foot and blisters may be the most familiar foot problems, but more serious and often ignored are the overuse injuries caused by stress on the many small bones which have to take the whole weight of the body. Good shoes are vital, but achieving the correct balance between sufficient protection and too much shoe weight is difficult. Orthotics may help correct some problems but must be fitted by an expert.

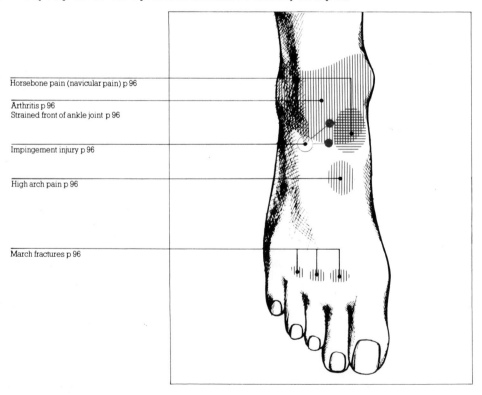

Horsebone pain (navicular pain) p 96

Arthritis p 96
Strained front of ankle joint p 96

Impingement injury p 96

High arch pain p 96

March fractures p 96

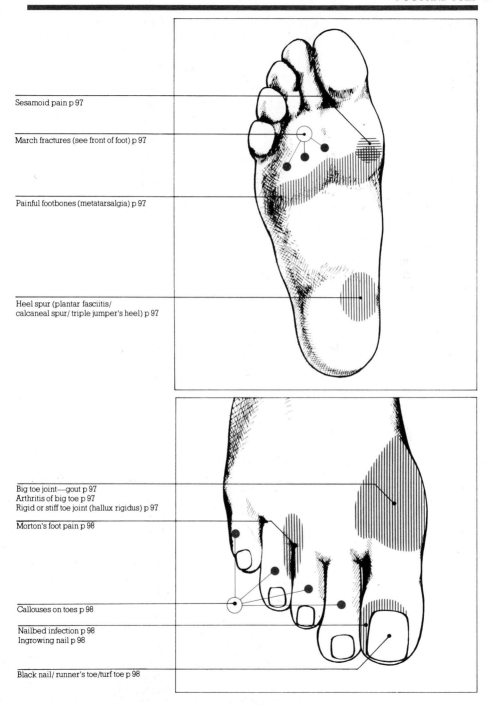

Sesamoid pain p 97

March fractures (see front of foot) p 97

Painful footbones (metatarsalgia) p 97

Heel spur (plantar fasciitis/
calcaneal spur/ triple jumper's heel) p 97

Big toe joint—gout p 97
Arthritis of big toe p 97
Rigid or stiff toe joint (hallux rigidus) p 97

Morton's foot pain p 98

Callouses on toes p 98

Nailbed infection p 98
Ingrowing nail p 98

Black nail/ runner's toe/turf toe p 98

ARTHRITIS

Diagnosis: May hurt at rest. Hurts to walk or run. *All* movements limited and painful at end of range. May cause swelling.

Cause: As cartilage wears down, bones roughen from grating together.

Treatment: *Self*—Rest. Aspirin.
Medical—Anti-inflammatory drugs. Shortwave diathermy. Cortisone injection. Surgery.

Training: Do not overexercise joint; space out training with rest intervals. May signal end of really active sports/games.

STRAINED FRONT OF ANKLE JOINT

Diagnosis: Most movements of ankle painless apart from forcing foot downwards.

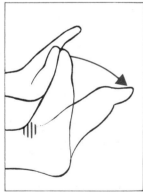

Cause: Strain of ligaments by sudden major, or repeated minor blows to foot. Forcing foot downwards (e.g. kicking a ball or having a kick blocked).

Treatment: *Self*—Rest. Aspirin. Double stirrup strapping (see p 89).
Medical—Prolonged rest. Shortwave diathermy. Ultrasound. Cross-frictional massage. Cortisone injection. Strapping.

Training: Continue as usual. Avoid kicking.

See: Soccer (chapter 5).

IMPINGEMENT INJURY

Diagnosis: Tender to touch near top part of foot. Hurts when foot forced up as far as possible.

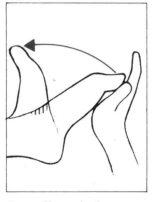

Cause: Upper footbones bang or impinge against shinbone, causing pain and sometimes producing spurs of bone which can fracture.

Treatment: *Self*—Rest.
Medical—Rest. Cortisone injection.

Training: Continue as usual.

See: Badminton, Gymnastics (chapter 5).

HORSEBONE PAIN (NAVICULAR PAIN)

Diagnosis: May hurt to walk, trot, run, but certainly when sprinting. Foot movements are painfree but pressure over upper inner footbone hurts.

Cause: Strain of same footbone that gives trouble in horses! May even produce stress fracture visible on X-ray, but it may only show on special scan.

Treatment: *Self*—Rest.
Medical—Rest. Plaster cast. May take 6 months or more to heal.

Training: **No** running. Swimming, bike, rowing routines. Try Achilles top ladder.

HIGH ARCH PAIN

Diagnosis: Pain and sometimes swelling on highest part of foot. Hurts to touch, but all foot movements painfree. Worse in shoes.

Cause: Pressure from last of shoe not cut with enough room for high arch.

Treatment: *Self*—Apply ice to affected part. Loosen laces. Get new pair of shoes or stretch old ones. Check shoe inserts or orthotics are not taking up too much space.
Medical—As above.

Training: Continue as usual.

MARCH FRACTURES

Diagnosis: Pain in central bones of forefoot when walking, marching (origin of name), trotting, running. Hurts to press relevant bone both from top and from sole of foot.

Cause: Stress fracture. Probably overuse in road running.

Treatment: *Self*—Rest. Use firm shoes for everyday wear which act like a splint around footbones; get shoes with really absorbent

soles and inners.
Medical—Rest. Rarely, plaster cast.
Training: Avoid running, even walking. Do swimming, bike, rowing routines. Try Achilles top ladder.

HEEL SPUR (PLANTAR FASCIITIS/CALCANEAL SPUR/TRIPLE JUMPER'S HEEL)

Diagnosis: Hurts under heel to walk or run. Painful to pressure. Half rising on ball of foot may hurt heel.
Cause: Strain of 'spring' ligament caused either by banging of heel or half stretch jump as in badminton smash. Spur of bone may be seen on X-ray but remains even when troublefree.
Treatment: *Self*—Rest. Insert shock-absorbent heel pads a good $\frac{1}{2}$ cm ($\frac{1}{4}$ in) thick when compressed. Firm heel cup. Aspirin. Also try arch support.
Medical—Rest. Heel pads. Podiatrist may use other methods. Cortisone injection. Anti-inflammatory drugs.
Training: Upper body work as usual. Swimming, rowing, bike, patter routines. Run when painfree.
See: Badminton, Track and field athletics (chapter 5).

PAINFUL FOOTBONES (METATARSALGIA)

Diagnosis: Painful bones on ball of foot, on running or walking. Hurts to press and may have prominent callous on skin.
Cause: Banging of foot on ground bruises more prominent bones—more common in high arch foot, claw toes and older people. Foot imbalance may cause pain under inside or outside of foot.
Treatment: *Self*—Cut pad of felt and place just heel side of forefoot bones. Pad lifts up forefoot, flattening claw toes—larger shoes may be needed as result!
Medical—Metatarsal pad. Orthotics. Surgery.
Training: Continue as usual unless painful.

SESAMOID PAIN

Diagnosis: Pain on ball of foot under great toe. Hurts to run or walk. Hurts to touch. Also hurts to resist gripping movement of big toe.
Cause: Banging or hard landing on small bone in tendon to big toe joint produces bruising or even fracture, especially in fast change of direction sports: tennis, squash, badminton, long and triple jumping.
Treatment: *Self*—Rest. Aspirin.
Medical—Anti-inflammatory drugs. Ultrasound. Cortisone injection. Plaster cast.
Training: Continue as usual unless painful.

MARCH FRACTURES

See p 96.

Toes

BIG TOE JOINT—GOUT

Diagnosis: Hot, swollen joint. Painful at rest and to move in any direction. NB This can occur in any joint in body.
Cause: Upset in body chemistry at any age—eating too much meat, perhaps, but not drinking port!
Treatment: *Self*—Rest. Seek medical advice.
Medical—Anti-gout drugs.
Training: Rest.

ARTHRITIS OF BIG TOE

Diagnosis: May be painful at rest. Walking and running may hurt. Hurts at end of range of all movements.
Cause: As cartilage wears down, bones roughen from grating together.
Treatment: *Self*—Rest. Aspirin. Warm bath. Run/walk with foot out and shorter stride to avoid rising up and over big toe; may have to alter to shuffle run.
Medical—Anti-inflammatory drugs. Shortwave diathermy. Cortisone injection. Surgery.
Training: Continue as usual.
See: Tennis (chapter 5).

RIGID OR STIFF TOE JOINT (HALLUX RIGIDUS)

Diagnosis: Big toe has little or no movement either up or down. May or may not be painful.
Cause: Big toe goes completely stiff.
Treatment: *Self*—As for Arthritis.
Medical—As for Arthritis.
Training: Continue as usual.
See: Tennis (chapter 5).

NAILBED INFECTION

Diagnosis: Red, painful, swollen, even with white or yellow area surrounding base and on side of nail.
Cause: Infection in skin.
Treatment: *Self*—Seek medical advice. Firm strapping may ease pain. Release pus by sterilizing needle in flame until red hot, cool and open skin *only* through yellow or white area. *Medical*—Drain pus. Antibiotics.
Training: Rest until cured.

INGROWING NAIL

Diagnosis: Pain, redness and discharge down side of nail and also near cut edge.
Cause: Nail edge damages skin, causing infection.
Treatment: *Self*—Cut nails square with very slight rounding; over-rounded nail may leave spear that grows into skin. Pack cotton wool (cotton balls) between nail and skin fold. Try to cut off spear of nail. Seek medical advice.
Medical—Antibiotics. Packing of nail. Surgery.
Training: Continue as usual.

BLACK NAIL/RUNNER'S TOE/TURF TOE

Diagnosis: Nail starts to turn black near base. May be painful. If this occurs rapidly, may be very painful and throbbing. Joint may also be swollen and painful; hurts in all movements.
Cause: 1 Shoe too short, or does not hold width of foot firmly so that foot slides forward and jams against end of shoe, especially on dry artificial turf.
2 Blow to toe may immediately bruise, causing blood under pressure beneath nail which is very painful. Nail later dies and grows out to drop off. Black area grows away from nailbed to end of nail.
Treatment: *Self*—Rest. ICE. Aspirin. Heat up pin/paper clip, hold in tweezers, burn hole in nail (doesn't hurt!), releasing spurt of blood; pain subsides. Try padding tongue of shoe with felt to stop forward slip of foot. Try new shoes.
Medical—Anti-inflammatory drugs. Shortwave diathermy. Drain blood through hole in nail as above. Antibiotics.
Training: Continue as usual.
See: Hockey (field), Squash (chapter 5).

CALLOUSES ON TOES

Diagnosis: Thickened pads on top of toe joints. See diagram of toes. Painful footbones.
Cause: Either claw toes or shoes too short.
Treatment: *Self*—Try metatarsal pad—see Painful footbones. Longer pair of shoes.
Medical—Metatarsal pad. Surgery.
Training: Continue as usual.

MORTON'S FOOT PAIN

Diagnosis: Burning pain down side of adjacent toes, usually 2nd and 3rd or 3rd and 4th.
Cause: Trapped nerve.
Treatment: *Self*—Arch support and pad under big toe.
Medical—Cortisone injection. Orthotics. Surgery.
Training: Continue as usual.

HOW TO RECOVER FROM AN INJURY
MALCOLM READ'S TRAINING LADDERS FOR REHABILITATION

Far too many sportsmen and women rush back too soon into action, impatient after even the shortest layoff. The result is often a recurrence of the problem, or, as the athlete tries to 'favour' the old injury, a new and different one.

The secret of a successful comeback is to put the injured area through a graduated series of exercises, each one a little more demanding than the last. This is the way in which the following 'training ladders' work. Starting on the bottom step of the ladder, the injured athlete works his or her way through these prescribed exercises. However, at the first sign of pain, the athlete must stop. If the pain or ache goes after 20 seconds, the exercises may be continued. However, if the ache or pain persists—STOP—WAIT 24 hours—BEGIN AGAIN FROM FIRST STEP.

No two injuries are alike, so the rate of healing will vary from person to person. By using these training ladders, any athlete can assess when he or she has done too much.

To find out which ladder plan is right for you, first diagnose your injury using the 'Top-to-Toe' section of this book. Correct treatment and training will be given there, referring you to the appropriate ladder plan if necessary.

Legs receive the most injuries, so there are several different ladders dealing with specific leg injuries. Some have two stages, a lower, then an upper ladder. The lower ladder is designed to keep you fit in the early stages of recovery, while the upper concentrates on rebuilding the strength and technique required by the legs. However, the lower should still be used after you have graduated to the upper ladder. Everyone from soccer players to basketball players and hockey players to sprinters can use these.

Other sports, like tennis, badminton, squash and baseball, require special ladders. These are also included. The general muscle ladder spells out the principles that apply to *any* injury—a step-by-step return to match fitness.

The special routines referred to in the ladder plans—e.g. patter, swimming, bike, etc.—are explained at the beginning of the section.

Remember: always stretch properly before exercises.

Patter routine

This simple exercise is immensely effective in raising pulse rate, building fitness yet not straining knees or hips. The secret is in *not* lifting the feet far off the ground. *Slow patter* is fast jogging on the spot with knees kept low. Feet must be lifted only 1–2 in off the floor. *Fast patter* is the same but as fast as you can.

ROUTINE FOR UNFIT ATHLETE (3 min)

1 min	slow patter
5 sec	fast patter
50 sec	slow patter
5 sec	fast patter
50 sec	slow patter
10 sec	fast patter

Rest for 3 min while doing stretching exercises.
Repeat above routine at least twice, preferably four times.

ROUTINE FOR FAIRLY FIT ATHLETE (5 min)

50 sec	slow patter
10 sec	fast patter
40 sec	slow patter
20 sec	fast patter
50 sec	slow patter
10 sec	fast patter
30 sec	slow patter
10 sec	fast patter
50 sec	slow patter
30 sec	fast patter

Rest for 3 min while doing stretching exercises.
Repeat above routine at least once, preferably three times.

ROUTINE FOR FIT ATHLETE (13 min)

Do routine for unfit athlete once, followed immediately by routine for fairly fit athlete twice.

Skipping routine

Use the same timing as the above patter routines, if you can skip that well! Try it at least, as it gives the calf muscles a good workout.

Swimming routine

Swimming is an excellent way of keeping the muscles toned up, especially when you cannot run. The water supports the body's weight but does not offer great resistance. Although less muscle power is required, the pulse rate is still raised by swimming.

ROUTINE FOR BAD SWIMMER

Jump in, swim or flounder across the width of the pool, climb out using good leg, stand up. Now turn around and repeat the routine for 3–5 min.
Rest for 3 min while doing stretching exercises.
Repeat above routine at least twice, preferably four times.

ROUTINE FOR GOOD SWIMMER

As above but swim one *length* each time.

Rowing routine

You need a rowing machine for this. It gives a thorough workout for legs, arms and abdominal muscles as well as building stamina. Untrained rowers will find this harder work than expected!

Make sure you:
1 Press equally hard with both legs. Try to get knees to travel at same rate, especially when locking them straight.
2 'Lie back' at end of stroke to exercise stomach muscle (if this is necessary).
3 Vary hand grip (either over top or underneath) if muscles ache.
4 Each machine has a different 'pull', so adjust your own routines accordingly.

ROUTINE FOR LONG-DISTANCE/STAMINA EVENTS

20 strokes per min for 5 min. Rest 3 min. Repeat as often as you like.

ROUTINE FOR MID-DISTANCE EVENTS AND RUNNING BALL GAMES

24–30 strokes per min for 3 min. Rest 3 min. Repeat as often as you like.

ROUTINE FOR SPRINT EVENTS AND MARTIAL ARTS

At least 30 strokes per min for 3 min. Rest 5 min. Repeat as often as you like.

Bike routine

This takes the pressure off leg joints and avoids jarring the back but still allows excellent work-out for heart and lungs. It may be done on a static exercise bike in a gym or on an ordinary pedal bike out on the road.

For stamina training: use easy, low gears at a pace where you are able to talk with only slight pant. For sprint training: use hard, higher gears. You are unable to talk.

ROUTINE FOR LONG-DISTANCE RUNNING

Your time on the bike should be equal to the time you would normally spend training on foot.

ROUTINE FOR MIDDLE-DISTANCE RUNNING AND BALL GAMES (5 min)

$4\frac{1}{2}$ min   stamina training
$\frac{1}{2}$ min   sprint training

Rest for 3 min while doing stretching exercises.
Repeat at least twice, preferably four times.

ROUTINE FOR SPRINT EVENTS, STRENGTH EVENTS, VOLLEYBALL, BASKETBALL, ETC. (5 min)

2 min   stamina training
15 sec   sprint training
1 min 45 sec   stamina training
1 min   sprint training

Rest for 4 min while doing stretching exercises.
Repeat at least twice, preferably four times.

General muscle ladder

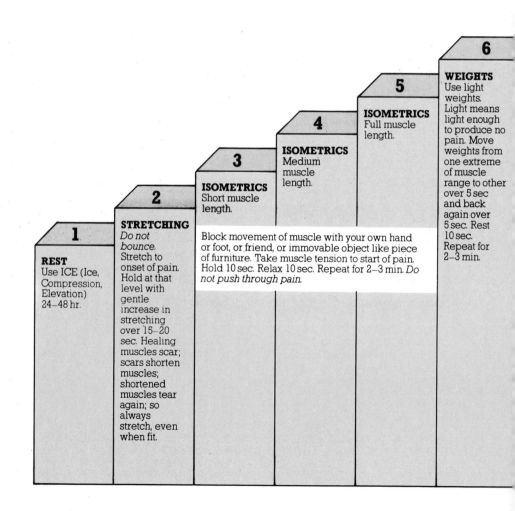

1

REST
Use ICE (Ice, Compression, Elevation) 24–48 hr.

2

STRETCHING
Do not bounce. Stretch to onset of pain. Hold at that level with gentle increase in stretching over 15–20 sec. Healing muscles scar; scars shorten muscles; shortened muscles tear again; so always stretch, even when fit.

3

ISOMETRICS
Short muscle length.

4

ISOMETRICS
Medium muscle length.

5

ISOMETRICS
Full muscle length.

6

WEIGHTS
Use light weights. Light means light enough to produce no pain. Move weights from one extreme of muscle range to other over 5 sec and back again over 5 sec. Rest 10 sec. Repeat for 2–3 min.

Block movement of muscle with your own hand or foot, or friend, or immovable object like piece of furniture. Take muscle tension to start of pain. Hold 10 sec. Relax 10 sec. Repeat for 2–3 min. *Do not push through pain.*

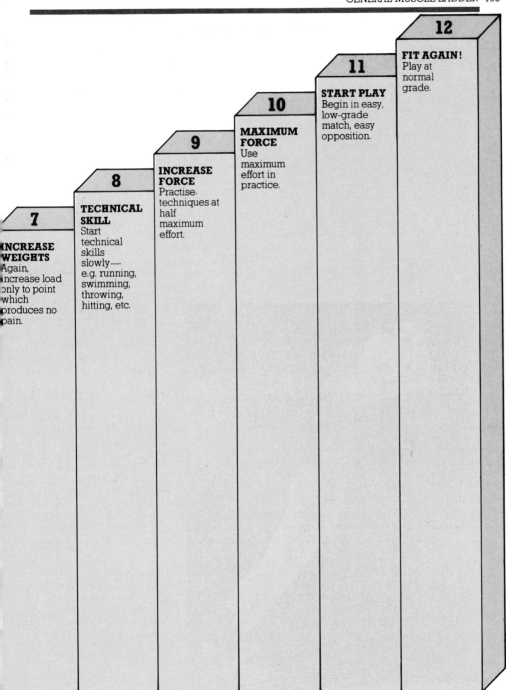

7

INCREASE WEIGHTS
Again, increase load only to point which produces no pain.

8

TECHNICAL SKILL
Start technical skills slowly—e.g. running, swimming, throwing, hitting, etc.

9

INCREASE FORCE
Practise techniques at half maximum effort.

10

MAXIMUM FORCE
Use maximum effort in practice.

11

START PLAY
Begin in easy, low-grade match, easy opposition.

12

FIT AGAIN!
Play at normal grade.

Quads ladder—Strength

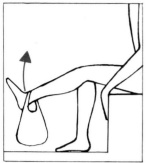

Step 2

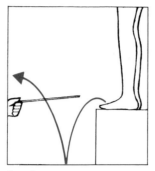

Step 8

6

SQUATS
If available, use weightlifting 'squat' technique. Use light weights, make sure knees never bend below 90°.

5

LEG PRESS MACHINE
If available, use leg press machine in gym with light weights.

4

SLOW STEP-UPS
Step up and back onto low bench or step, alternating feet.

3

SKIER'S EXERCISE
'Sit' with back against wall, thighs parallel to ground. Do not drop below horizontal. Hold 10 sec. Rest 10 sec. Repeat 6 times.

2

KNEE STRAIGHT-ENING
Supporting upper leg of injured knee on bench, in hands, or on fit leg, sit with carrier bag or basket containing 2 kg (4½ lb) over ankle of injured leg. (Use sugar, canned soup, etc.) Raise and straighten leg. Hold 10 sec. Repeat 6 times.

1

ISOMETRICS
Standing up, lock injured knee straight, tense thigh muscles. Hold 10 sec. Repeat 6 times.

7

BIKE ROUTINE
(p 103)
Use high gear, low pedal rate. Continue until muscle aches. Rest 5–10 min. Repeat as fitness allows.

8

DEPTH JUMPS
Jump down from low step (15–20 cm/ 6–8 in) then up over string or bar (like high jump bar). Find highest you can jump. Drop this height by 5 cm (2 in), then repeat 10 times. Jump rhythmically down and over with no bounce in between. Start with *both* legs. Eventually improve to single-leg jumps. Over the weeks gradually raise height of step by placing, say, large book on it.

9

HOP, STEP, JUMP
Idea is to travel as *far* as you can. As this is measurable, you can have competitions with other athletes. *Start* with right toe on line, *hop* onto right foot, *step* onto left foot, *jump* from left foot, land on both feet. Mark how far you have reached. Repeat, starting from left foot. Do 5 times each foot.

10

WEIGHTS
Resume normal weight-training to level before injury.

Quads ladder—Heart & lungs

The heart & lungs ladder builds up your stamina. To rebuild muscle strength, use the strength ladder. These two may be worked in parallel. However, competitors in 'power' events should concentrate on strength, while 'speed' and 'endurance' competitors will find the heart & lungs ladder more appropriate. Competitors in most ball games will use both ladders.

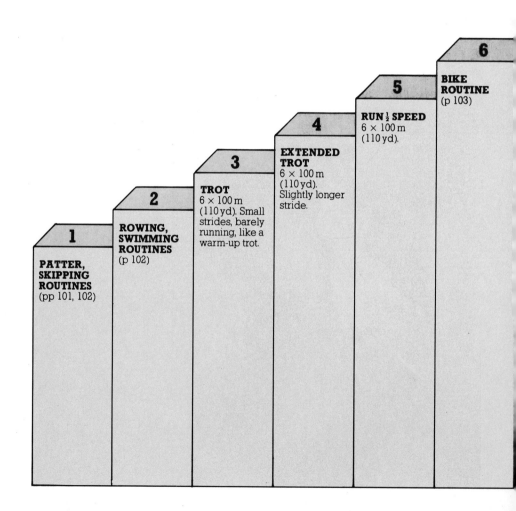

1
PATTER, SKIPPING ROUTINES (pp 101, 102)

2
ROWING, SWIMMING ROUTINES (p 102)

3
TROT 6 × 100 m (110 yd). Small strides, barely running, like a warm-up trot.

4
EXTENDED TROT 6 × 100 m (110 yd). Slightly longer stride.

5
RUN ½ SPEED 6 × 100 m (110 yd).

6
BIKE ROUTINE (p 103)

7

RUN ¾ SPEED
6 × 100 m
(110 yd). Do not
increase stride
length beyond
normal.

8

SPRINT
6 × 100 m
(110 yd). Full
speed.

9

START PLAY
Begin in easy,
low-grade
match, easy
opposition.

10

FIT AGAIN!
Play at normal
grade.

Knee ladder

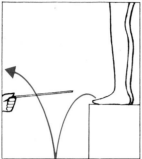

Step 5

Strapping: Knee should be supported (strapped) through all of this ladder and first 6 weeks of match play.

When you can sprint 100 m (110 yd) without pain (i.e. at top of Achilles or hamstring ladder) start here.

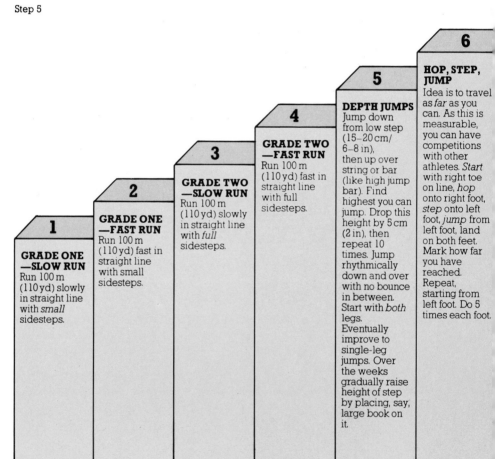

1

GRADE ONE —SLOW RUN
Run 100 m (110 yd) slowly in straight line with *small* sidesteps.

2

GRADE ONE —FAST RUN
Run 100 m (110 yd) fast in straight line with small sidesteps.

3

GRADE TWO —SLOW RUN
Run 100 m (110 yd) slowly in straight line with *full* sidesteps.

4

GRADE TWO —FAST RUN
Run 100 m (110 yd) fast in straight line with full sidesteps.

5

DEPTH JUMPS
Jump down from low step (15–20 cm/ 6–8 in), then up over string or bar (like high jump bar). Find highest you can jump. Drop this height by 5 cm (2 in), then repeat 10 times. Jump rhythmically down and over with no bounce in between. Start with *both* legs. Eventually improve to single-leg jumps. Over the weeks gradually raise height of step by placing, say, large book on it.

6

HOP, STEP, JUMP
Idea is to travel as *far* as you can. As this is measurable, you can have competitions with other athletes. *Start* with right toe on line, *hop* onto right foot, *step* onto left foot, *jump* from left foot, land on both feet. Mark how far you have reached. Repeat, starting from left foot. Do 5 times each foot.

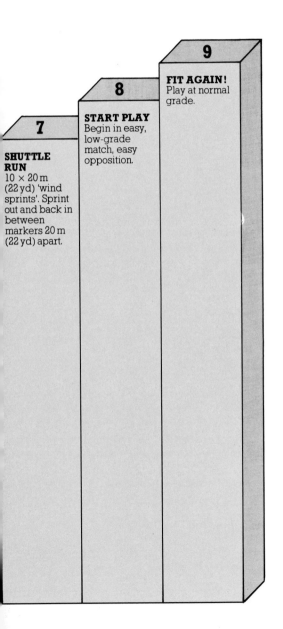

7

SHUTTLE RUN
$10 \times 20\,m$ (22 yd) 'wind sprints'. Sprint out and back in between markers 20 m (22 yd) apart.

8

START PLAY
Begin in easy, low-grade match, easy opposition.

9

FIT AGAIN!
Play at normal grade.

Calf & Achilles bottom ladder

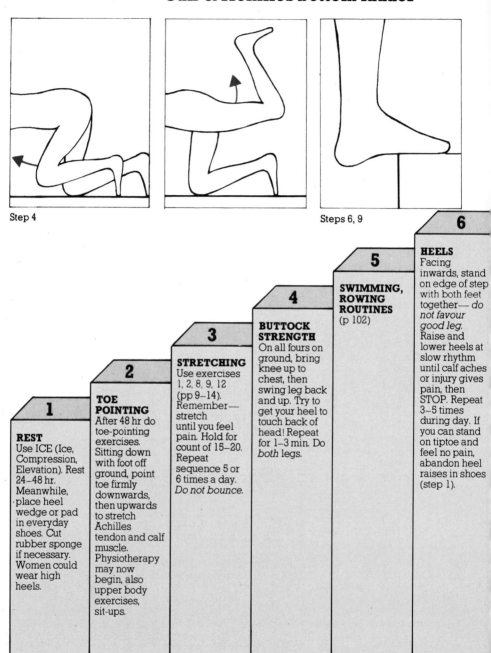

Step 4

Steps 6, 9

1

REST
Use ICE (Ice, Compression, Elevation). Rest 24–48 hr. Meanwhile, place heel wedge or pad in everyday shoes. Cut rubber sponge if necessary. Women could wear high heels.

2

TOE POINTING
After 48 hr do toe-pointing exercises. Sitting down with foot off ground, point toe firmly downwards, then upwards to stretch Achilles tendon and calf muscle. Physiotherapy may now begin, also upper body exercises, sit-ups.

3

STRETCHING
Use exercises 1, 2, 8, 9, 12 (pp 9–14). Remember—stretch until you feel pain. Hold for count of 15–20. Repeat sequence 5 or 6 times a day. *Do not bounce.*

4

BUTTOCK STRENGTH
On all fours on ground, bring knee up to chest, then swing leg back and up. Try to get your heel to touch back of head! Repeat for 1–3 min. Do *both* legs.

5

SWIMMING, ROWING ROUTINES (p 102)

6

HEELS
Facing inwards, stand on edge of step with both feet together— *do not favour good leg.* Raise and lower heels at slow rhythm until calf aches or injury gives pain, then STOP. Repeat 3–5 times during day. If you can stand on tiptoe and feel no pain, abandon heel raises in shoes (step 1).

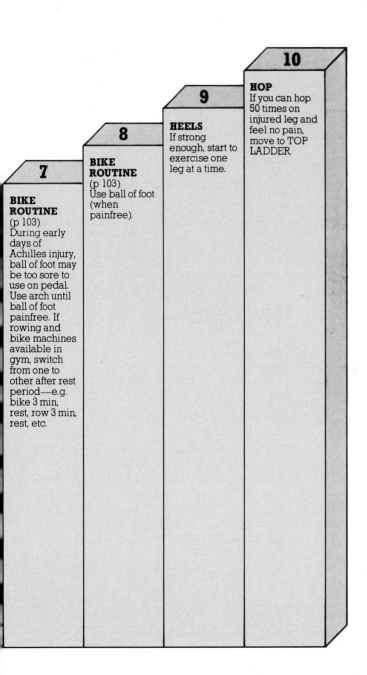

7

BIKE ROUTINE
(p 103)
During early days of Achilles injury, ball of foot may be too sore to use on pedal. Use arch until ball of foot painfree. If rowing and bike machines available in gym, switch from one to other after rest period—e.g. bike 3 min, rest, row 3 min, rest, etc.

8

BIKE ROUTINE
(p 103)
Use ball of foot (when painfree).

9

HEELS
If strong enough, start to exercise one leg at a time.

10

HOP
If you can hop 50 times on injured leg and feel no pain, move to TOP LADDER.

Calf & Achilles top ladder

Start again from beginning at each training session but early ladder steps may be cut from 6 times to 3 times. Continue using BOTTOM LADDER for fitness. Check that leg rhythm is always equal; do not 'gallop'. One way to avoid favouring injured leg is to count out loud from 1 to 10 while running. This sets rhythm for legs to follow. Counting 1, 2; 1, 2 tends to stress any limp. Stretch between each 100 m (110 yd). Check knee lift and heel pick-up are same height.

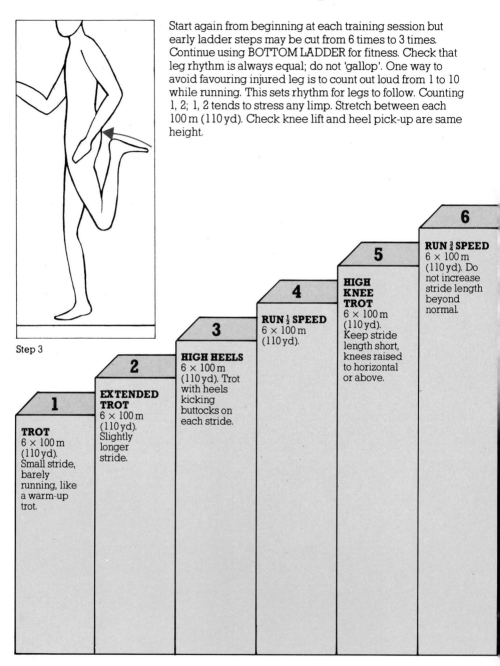

Step 3

1

TROT
6 × 100 m (110 yd). Small stride, barely running, like a warm-up trot.

2

EXTENDED TROT
6 × 100 m (110 yd). Slightly longer stride.

3

HIGH HEELS
6 × 100 m (110 yd). Trot with heels kicking buttocks on each stride.

4

RUN ½ SPEED
6 × 100 m (110 yd).

5

HIGH KNEE TROT
6 × 100 m (110 yd). Keep stride length short, knees raised to horizontal or above.

6

RUN ¾ SPEED
6 × 100 m (110 yd). Do not increase stride length beyond normal.

7

GRADE ONE SPRINT
6 × 100 m (110 yd). Accelerate 25 m (27 yd); sprint 50 m (55 yd); slow down 25 m (27 yd).

8

GRADE TWO SPRINT
6 × 100 m (110 yd). Accelerate 25 m (27 yd); sprint 50 m (55 yd); fast stop 25 m (27 yd).

9

GRADE THREE SPRINT
6 × 100 m (110 yd). Fast accelerate 25 m (27 yd); sprint 50 m (55 yd); fast stop 25 m (27 yd).

10

SHUTTLE RUN
10 × 20 m (22 yd) 'wind sprints'. Sprint out and back in between markers 20 m (22 yd) apart.

11

START PLAY
Begin in easy, low-grade match, easy opposition.

12

FIT AGAIN!
Play at normal grade.

NB Specialist runners should still use 'slow' stop (step 7). 'Fast' stop is only for 'stop-start' sports, usually ball games.

Hamstring bottom ladder

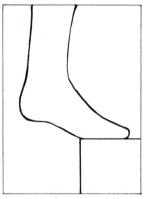

Step 5

Strapping: If the *knee* is injured, it should be supported (strapped) through all of this ladder and first 6 weeks of match play.

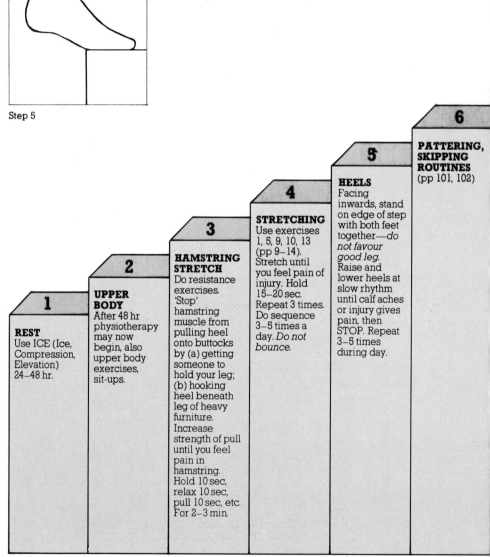

1

REST
Use ICE (Ice, Compression, Elevation) 24–48 hr.

2

UPPER BODY
After 48 hr physiotherapy may now begin, also upper body exercises, sit-ups.

3

HAMSTRING STRETCH
Do resistance exercises. 'Stop' hamstring muscle from pulling heel onto buttocks by (a) getting someone to hold your leg; (b) hooking heel beneath leg of heavy furniture. Increase strength of pull until you feel pain in hamstring. Hold 10 sec, relax 10 sec, pull 10 sec, etc. For 2–3 min.

4

STRETCHING
Use exercises 1, 5, 9, 10, 13 (pp 9–14). Stretch until you feel pain of injury. Hold 15–20 sec. Repeat 3 times. Do sequence 3–5 times a day. *Do not bounce.*

5

HEELS
Facing inwards, stand on edge of step with both feet together—*do not favour good leg.* Raise and lower heels at slow rhythm until calf aches or injury gives pain, then STOP. Repeat 3–5 times during day.

6

PATTERING, SKIPPING ROUTINES
(pp 101, 102)

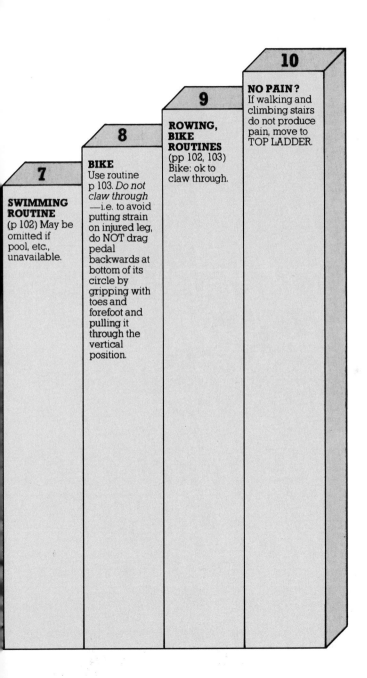

7

SWIMMING ROUTINE (p 102) May be omitted if pool, etc., unavailable.

8

BIKE Use routine p 103. *Do not claw through* —i.e. to avoid putting strain on injured leg, do NOT drag pedal backwards at bottom of its circle by gripping with toes and forefoot and pulling it through the vertical position.

9

ROWING, BIKE ROUTINES (pp 102, 103) Bike: ok to claw through.

10

NO PAIN? If walking and climbing stairs do not produce pain, move to TOP LADDER.

Hamstring top ladder

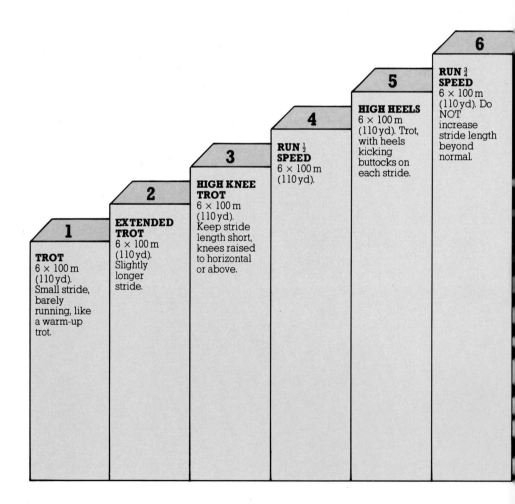

1

TROT
6 × 100 m
(110 yd).
Small stride,
barely
running, like
a warm-up
trot.

2

**EXTENDED
TROT**
6 × 100 m
(110 yd).
Slightly
longer
stride.

3

**HIGH KNEE
TROT**
6 × 100 m
(110 yd).
Keep stride
length short,
knees raised
to horizontal
or above.

4

**RUN $\frac{1}{2}$
SPEED**
6 × 100 m
(110 yd).

5

HIGH HEELS
6 × 100 m
(110 yd). Trot,
with heels
kicking
buttocks on
each stride.

6

**RUN $\frac{3}{4}$
SPEED**
6 × 100 m
(110 yd). Do
NOT
increase
stride length
beyond
normal.

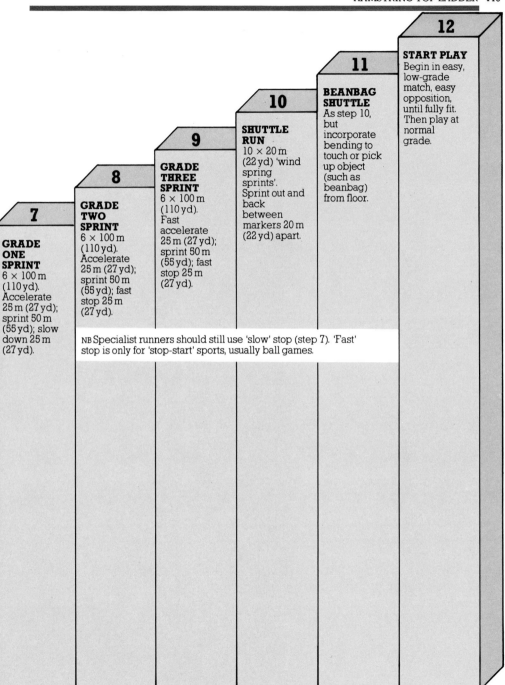

12

START PLAY
Begin in easy, low-grade match, easy opposition, until fully fit. Then play at normal grade.

11

BEANBAG SHUTTLE
As step 10, but incorporate bending to touch or pick up object (such as beanbag) from floor.

10

SHUTTLE RUN
10 × 20 m (22 yd) 'wind spring sprints'. Sprint out and back between markers 20 m (22 yd) apart.

9

GRADE THREE SPRINT
6 × 100 m (110 yd). Fast accelerate 25 m (27 yd); sprint 50 m (55 yd); fast stop 25 m (27 yd).

8

GRADE TWO SPRINT
6 × 100 m (110 yd). Accelerate 25 m (27 yd); sprint 50 m (55 yd); fast stop 25 m (27 yd).

7

GRADE ONE SPRINT
6 × 100 m (110 yd). Accelerate 25 m (27 yd); sprint 50 m (55 yd); slow down 25 m (27 yd).

NB Specialist runners should still use 'slow' stop (step 7). 'Fast' stop is only for 'stop-start' sports, usually ball games.

Badminton ladder

Find a willing partner/opponent who will provide you with the necessary shots. Work 5 min at each level. As you move up ladder repeat lower steps as part of training routine. Remember, at the first sign of pain you must stop. If the pain or ache goes after 20 sec, continue the exercises. However, if the ache or pain persists— STOP—WAIT 24 hours—begin again from first step.

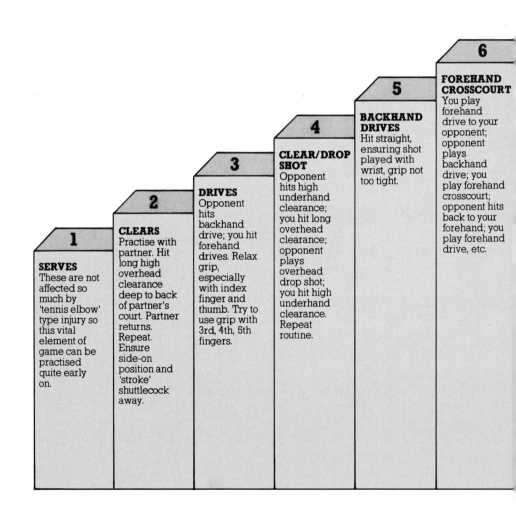

1

SERVES
These are not affected so much by 'tennis elbow' type injury so this vital element of game can be practised quite early on.

2

CLEARS
Practise with partner. Hit long high overhead clearance deep to back of partner's court. Partner returns. Repeat. Ensure side-on position and 'stroke' shuttlecock away.

3

DRIVES
Opponent hits backhand drive; you hit forehand drives. Relax grip, especially with index finger and thumb. Try to use grip with 3rd, 4th, 5th fingers.

4

CLEAR/DROP SHOT
Opponent hits high underhand clearance; you hit long overhead clearance; opponent plays overhead drop shot; you hit high underhand clearance. Repeat routine.

5

BACKHAND DRIVES
Hit straight, ensuring shot played with wrist, grip not too tight.

6

FOREHAND CROSSCOURT
You play forehand drive to your opponent; opponent plays backhand drive; you play forehand crosscourt; opponent hits back to your forehand; you play forehand drive, etc.

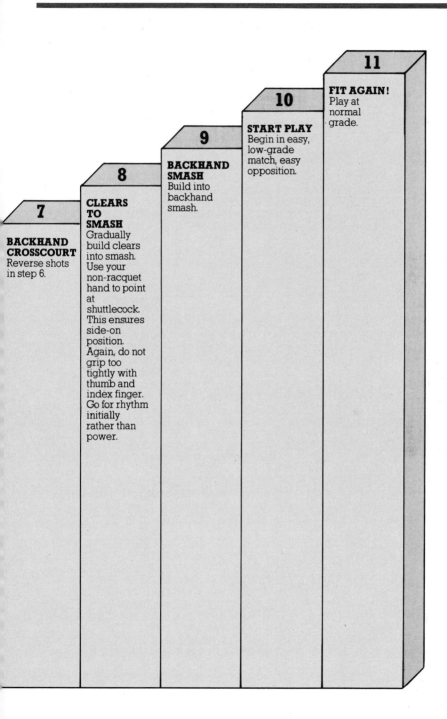

7

BACKHAND CROSSCOURT
Reverse shots in step 6.

8

CLEARS TO SMASH
Gradually build clears into smash. Use your non-racquet hand to point at shuttlecock. This ensures side-on position. Again, do not grip too tightly with thumb and index finger. Go for rhythm initially rather than power.

9

BACKHAND SMASH
Build into backhand smash.

10

START PLAY
Begin in easy, low-grade match, easy opposition.

11

FIT AGAIN!
Play at normal grade.

Tennis ladder

Find a willing partner/opponent who will provide you with the necessary shots, or use a tennis machine. Work on technique. Concentrate on footwork and getting sideways onto ball. When playing singlehanded backhand make sure racquet head stays above wrist level; do not 'lead' with elbow. Check with coach if available. Do not 'snatch' at shots. Work 5 min at each level. As you move up ladder repeat lower steps as part of training routine. Remember, at the first sign of pain you must stop. If the pain or ache goes after 20 sec, continue the exercises. However, if the ache or pain persists—STOP—WAIT 24 hours—begin again from first step.

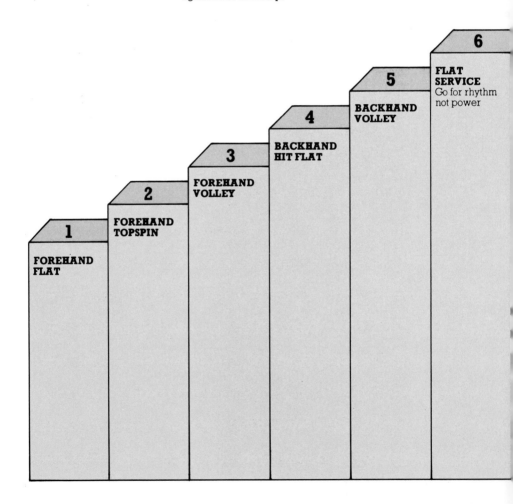

1 FOREHAND FLAT

2 FOREHAND TOPSPIN

3 FOREHAND VOLLEY

4 BACKHAND HIT FLAT

5 BACKHAND VOLLEY

6 FLAT SERVICE Go for rhythm not power

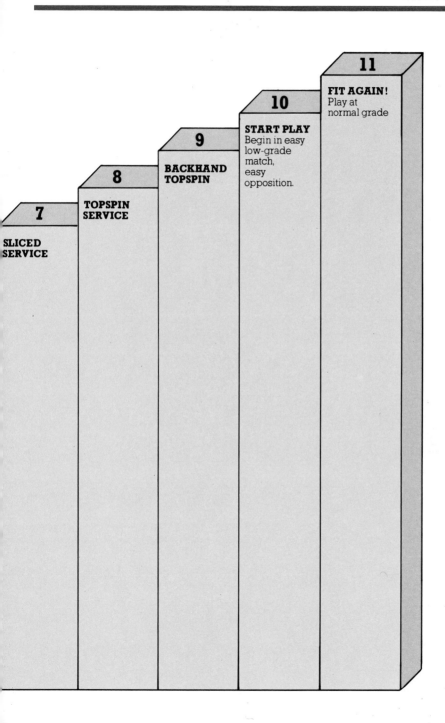

7

SLICED SERVICE

8

TOPSPIN SERVICE

9

BACKHAND TOPSPIN

10

START PLAY
Begin in easy low-grade match, easy opposition.

11

FIT AGAIN!
Play at normal grade

Squash ladder

Find a willing partner/opponent who will provide you with the necessary shots. Work 5 min at each level. As you move up ladder repeat lower steps as part of training routine. Remember, at the first sign of pain you must stop. If the pain or ache goes after 20 sec, continue the exercises. However, if the ache or pain persists—STOP—WAIT 24 hours—begin again from first step.

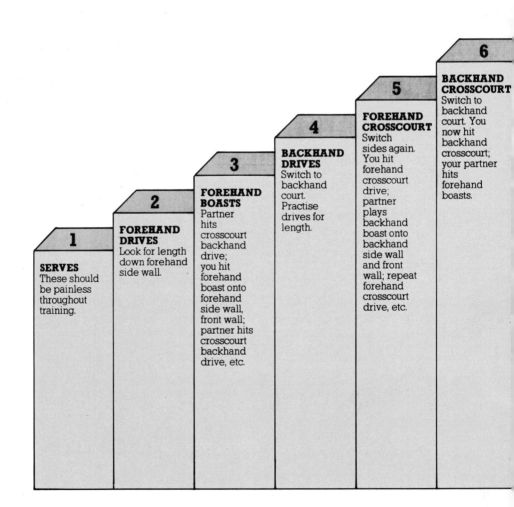

1

SERVES
These should be painless throughout training.

2

FOREHAND DRIVES
Look for length down forehand side wall.

3

FOREHAND BOASTS
Partner hits crosscourt backhand drive; you hit forehand boast onto forehand side wall, front wall; partner hits crosscourt backhand drive, etc.

4

BACKHAND DRIVES
Switch to backhand court. Practise drives for length.

5

FOREHAND CROSSCOURT
Switch sides again. You hit forehand crosscourt drive; partner plays backhand boast onto backhand side wall and front wall; repeat forehand crosscourt drive, etc.

6

BACKHAND CROSSCOURT
Switch to backhand court. You now hit backhand crosscourt; your partner hits forehand boasts.

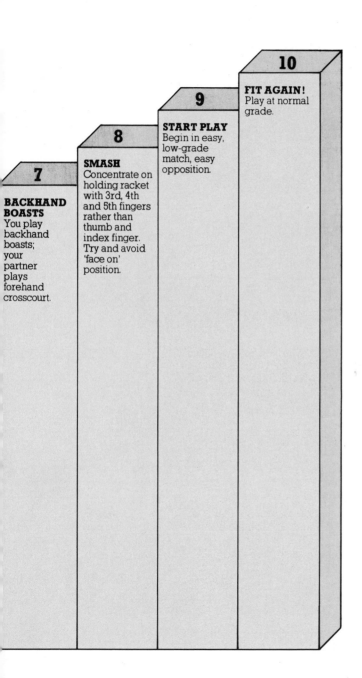

10

FIT AGAIN!
Play at normal grade.

9

START PLAY
Begin in easy, low-grade match, easy opposition.

8

SMASH
Concentrate on holding racket with 3rd, 4th and 5th fingers rather than thumb and index finger. Try and avoid 'face on' position.

7

BACKHAND BOASTS
You play backhand boasts; your partner plays forehand crosscourt.

Baseball ladder

Find a willing partner. Work 5 min at each level. As you move up ladder, repeat lower steps as part of training routine. Remember, at the first sign of pain you must stop. If the pain or ache goes after 20 sec, continue the exercises. However, if the ache or pain persists—STOP—WAIT 24 hours—begin again from first step.

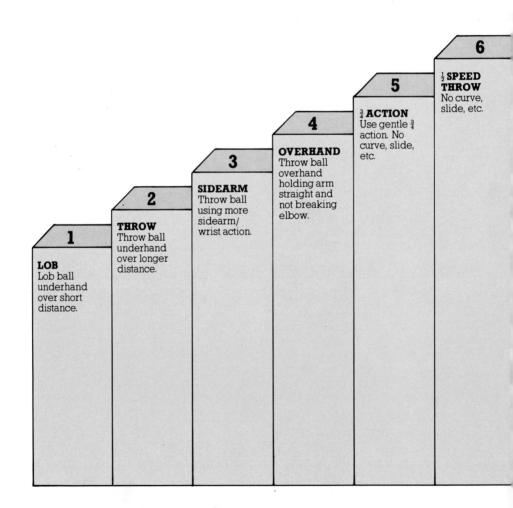

1

LOB
Lob ball underhand over short distance.

2

THROW
Throw ball underhand over longer distance.

3

SIDEARM
Throw ball using more sidearm/wrist action.

4

OVERHAND
Throw ball overhand holding arm straight and not breaking elbow.

5

$\frac{3}{4}$ **ACTION**
Use gentle $\frac{3}{4}$ action. No curve, slide, etc.

6

$\frac{1}{2}$ **SPEED THROW**
No curve, slide, etc.

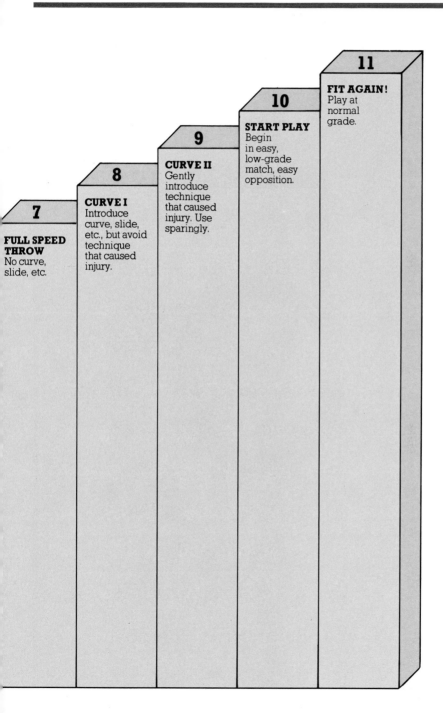

7

FULL SPEED THROW
No curve, slide, etc.

8

CURVE I
Introduce curve, slide, etc., but avoid technique that caused injury.

9

CURVE II
Gently introduce technique that caused injury. Use sparingly.

10

START PLAY
Begin in easy, low-grade match, easy opposition.

11

FIT AGAIN!
Play at normal grade.

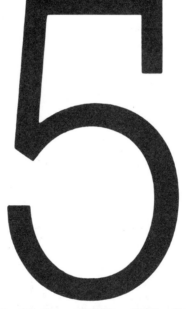

SPORT-BY-SPORT GUIDE TO TECHNICAL INJURIES

Every sport in the world makes different demands on the participants. Some require endurance, others speed. Some need great flexibility, others great technical skill. In this sport-by-sport rundown, you can spot the peculiarities of your own particular sport, so that you are better prepared to avoid injuries—or to recognize them if you are unlucky enough to suffer them. Injuries that are explained in the Top-to-Toe Guide (chapter 3) are in heavy type.

Archery	Archers are not prone to serious injuries, but can avoid annoying ones by using equipment tailored to their needs. The bow must obviously be the correct weight because too heavy a drawweight can be tiring. Finger tabs should·suit the individual, so new ones should be cut to the right shape and size under the guidance of a coach. And fingers can suffer if the correct technique of holding the string is not employed. Chest protectors and arm braces must be worn, and as archers get older and lose flexibility they may, with a coach's help, have to adapt technique and drawweight.

Tennis elbow can occur in the arm holding the bow when the wrist is extended through the draw before locking it into the support position. This may help the draw, but could mean the drawweight is too heavy. **Biceps strain** from using too heavy a drawweight can be healed after a proper rest. Technique should be checked by a coach and training resumed with a lighter bow. |
| **Badminton** | At top level, one of the most demanding sports. Footwear is important, as many matches are played on firm, composition floors rather than better sprung, wooden surfaces. Properly padded shoes absorb shock and help prevent blisters and forefoot strains. The knee on the racquet-hand side is susceptible to great stresses. Although pain is common in the wrists and shoulders, this is often due to poor footwork. Striking the shuttle when in an awkward, off-balance position strains the joints. Correct technique not only makes shots more effective, but also avoids injury.

A/C joint injury could take you out for the rest of the season, since overhead shots flare the condition. As below-the-shoulder shots are all right, try squash during |

the lay-off period and seek medical advice.

Painful arc or **Subacromial joint injuries** need to be diagnosed accurately if the technical fault is to be corrected. Caused by hitting too hard 'with the shoulder' or smashing from too far behind the head, their best treatment is to reduce the power of the shot and hit with the wrist. Check with a coach that you are not smashing 'face on', and that your feet are correctly positioned. Early cortisone injections are of value, and in severe cases fitness can be maintained by playing squash. The shuttle moves at anything between 5 and 90 mph (8–150 kph), so coaches emphasize the importance of correct technique. Incorrect lunging can cause severe lower back and/or even hamstring area problems. To avoid Achilles tendon problems in the trailing leg, the scissors kick must be executed correctly.

Sufferers from **Adductor muscle strain** should avoid overstretching sideways when building back into competition. The 'round the head' shot may inflame the sartorius muscle.

Players suffering from **Pulled quads, Quads expansion, Chondromalacia, Jumper's knee, Lower pole strain** or **Osgood Schlatter's disease** should avoid reaching over the knee during training to pick up drop shots. Only play shuttlecock above the waist until painfree and reduce quads training.

Impingement injuries of the ankle occur in the trail leg from deep lunging, so check footwork. Turn trail foot out sideways (as fencers do) rather than lunge over a toes-forward straight foot. If there is a 'popping' feeling in the lead-leg knee when lunging forward, a major internal ligament could well have torn. See **Unstable knee** and **Rapid swelling**: seek early medical advice.

A **Pull-off fracture of the thigh** is produced by repeated lunging, which loads the quads; this is common in growing youngsters. Seek medical advice. **Tennis elbow** is common, especially in doubles, where the net player has to angle forehand interceptions. If the grip is too tight (using the thumb and index finger) the wrist is not released enough to angle the shot, so the elbow is jammed straight, flaring the radio-humeral joint. Check your grip with a coach; try a thicker grip and hold with the third, fourth and fifth fingers. Another cause is the tendency to come face onto the smash, then whipping the shot with the wrist. See **Badminton ladder plan. Plantar fasciitis** is common on non-sprung floors, and even half-rising on the toes when preparing to smash may hurt. Concentrate on pattering for fitness while running is painful.

Baseball/Softball

As in the British equivalent, cricket, baseball players never seem to be as fit as they could and should be. In a game involving sudden moves after long periods of inaction, hamstrings are likely to go in the sprint for first base and groin pulls occur in attempting awkward ground balls, so thorough warm-ups and stretching are vital.

The most well-known injury is **Pitcher's elbow**, which covers a multitude of sins but is mainly due to fast snapping of the elbow into extension, especially if wrist cock is maintained throughout delivery, as in 'change up'. **Olecranon fossa, Olecranon fracture** and **Triceps strain** can all be caused by the strain of snapping the elbow straight when delivering the fastball and change up, plus insufficient forearm strength to cope. A **Radio-humeral joint** sprain can be flared by pitching the screwball, so avoid overusing this delivery if causing problems. **Golfer's elbow**, a type of pitcher's elbow, is an overuse injury, caused by trying to gain more speed on the fastball and when pitching the curveball or slider. Both of these release the cocked wrist through delivery, and threequarter action increases the risk of this injury.

Little league elbow/pull-off fracture is one of the problems of the sport where overenthusiastic youngsters (or worse, youngsters encouraged by overenthusiastic parents) are allowed to damage themselves by repeatedly throwing fastballs. It is interesting to note that round-arm javelin-throwing produces this selfsame injury, and it is possible that the threequarter action (more common in beginners) plays a part. As the bones are still growing, any elbow injury must be treated seriously and by medical experts—there is the risk that growth may be permanently impaired. Most pitching by youngsters is supervised to control the number of pitches per week, and many coaches forbid the throwing of curved balls. Technique, accuracy and control should be encouraged as opposed to speed. As soon as a youngster says, 'It hurts when I throw', stop play, seek medical advice.

If throwing is painless sidearm but painful overarm, the chances are that it is a **Shoulder separation/A/C joint grade I** injury. **Shoulder impingement/subacromial bursa** injury can occur when fielders attempt to throw too hard overarm. Throw side or underarm. Treat early with cortisone injections. It is worth remembering that good lower body strength can help the upper body by taking some of the strain off the arm through proper takeoff and followthrough.

Jammed fingers are common. See a doctor if out of line and tape to a healthy finger for support. **Mallet** or **baseball finger** is more serious, as the tip of the finger droops and cannot be straightened. This needs splinting by a doctor.

Sliding techniques are important—but can anyone agree on the 'correct' method? Putting the full weight of the body at speed onto an ankle that is resisted by a rough surface is asking for trouble—so one school of thought suggests headfirst slides into second and third base. As the catcher is a pretty solid object, feet first is advisable at home plate. Whether your coach accepts this or not, everyone agrees that indecision is the worst decision!

Basketball/Handball/ Netball/Volleyball

Feet, knees and ankles are a problem when these sports are played on firm surfaces, so footwear must be well padded to reduce risk from jumping and landing, checking and changing direction. As the hands have to deal with a large ball, **Mallet finger**, **Sprained thumb** and **Dislocated finger** injuries are inherent problems, and strapping of joints is both beneficial and preventative. Correct catching technique helps in basketball, for example, where the 'block and grab' method is encouraged. Instead of catching the ball two-handed with the thumbs together at the back, hold up one hand to receive the ball and complete the catch by bringing the other hand round in front.

Because taller players have a higher centre of gravity, **Ankle sprains** are common due to sharp changes of direction. Many coaches insist on routine ankle strapping, but this only transfers the strain to the area of the knee. Basketball and handball players could suffer from **Footballer's groin** as they twist from side to side whilst backing off in defence. Maintain shooting skills from a static position and build up gradually to running shots. Coaches should use players in zonal rather than man-to-man defence play to allow recovery.

Jumper's leg is common, so correct jumping technique is important for beginners. **Jumper's knee** is another inherent problem in all four sports, but handballers are particularly susceptible to shoulder-throwing injuries (**Shoulder separation/A/C joint, Shoulder impingement/subacromial bursa, Painful arc**).

Bowling, Tenpin

Scarcely the most energetic sport, it still produces some peculiar afflictions, such as **Bowler's elbow**, from the sheer weight of the ball. ICE and rest are advised. Check the weight and correct drilling of holes in a personalized ball for the frequent participant. **Bowler's toe** afflicts as many as a third of all bowlers due to the stress placed on the big and second toes of the trailing foot on delivery. Check footwear to avoid misshapen toes, thickened toenails and callouses. Keep the elbow tucked in or the whole arm will finish across and in front of the body, straining the shoulder. Thumb irritation and callouses are common among regular bowlers. Cover sore areas and sand down callouses.

Bowls

Another gentle sport, where only the onset of old age together with arthritis dictates a change of technique. Concentration on the back strain position on delivery will prevent further problems.

Boxing

Apart from the obvious pummelling that the head, hands and upper body take, there is damage peculiar to the sport such as **Cut eyes**. Dilute adrenalin may be used during the bout, but it is essential that early pressure and ice are applied and (if needed) sutures rather than adhesive stitches to give the best results. The suturing (stitching) should be under the skin, with great care being taken to 'approximate' the edges of the wound. Enzyme creams minimize scarring but three weeks are needed for skin to regain its normal strength, even if it appears to be healed much sooner: always use head guards for sparring. After a **Knockout/KO**, amateur boxers are not allowed to fight again for 28 days (first time), 84 days (second time) and one year (third time). The risk is 'punch drunkenness' (brain damage), and regular brain (CAT) scans are now part of professional boxing. If a boxer is shortsighted (nearsighted) he should beware, because there is a proven connection between myopia and an increased likelihood of a detached retina. This can cause blindness. Do not 'risk it'. The only solution is to give up boxing.

Repeated punching can develop a small spur of bone in the muscle tendon just above the elbow. A direct blow can break it off, causing pain (**Boxer's arm**) in the upper arm. This is confirmed by resisting an upward movement of the forearm (fist clenched, thumb on top). After 4–6 weeks' rest the spur will reattach itself, but may need surgical removal.

Five per cent weight loss by dehydration causes 20–30 per cent drop in work rate. Try to train at fighting weight.

Canoeing and Kayaking

'Messing about on the water' is an obvious risk, so basic safety drill must always be employed—even by the best swimmers. Anything more demanding than the shortest leisure trips requires a good standard of fitness and proper technique to avoid aches and pains.

Hypothermia (see under Some sensible tips (chapter 1)) is a major risk: be prepared. Although wildwater paddlers prepare for this, K2, K3 and K4 often forget how cold paddle splashes can be. Use a body wetsuit (low cut under arms, loose rubber/plastic sleeves) in cold conditions when training. Remember—energy spent warming the body is not available for muscle effort!

Paddler's wrist is common in kayakers, who feel pain on the lower end of the forearm when extending the wrist and hand in a 'claw' position (as if paddling or rowing); the long tendon and sheath of the thumb are inflamed in the wrist and forearm. Cross-frictional massage, ultrasound and an injection of cortisone may help, but surgery may be required to release constriction of the sheath.

Also, **Biceps tendinitis** can occur (more in the shoulder than the elbow) due to overuse. Check with a coach in case your pull/twist technique is faulty. **Tennis elbow** is often caused by lack of forearm strength to take strain as well as faulty technique. See a coach.

Many aches and pains can be corrected by checking width of grip (upper body strains) and placement of the seat in relation to the footrest/rudder control (lower back). Twisting strain on the back is likely to flare upper back pain, so seek manipulation early. And hunching to increase power overloads the midback, so make sure the back strain position is second nature before increasing paddling thrust.

Novice canoeists can suffer **Housemaid's knee** from kneeling, so use a polystyrene pad lined with sheepskin as protection and give the knee a chance to adapt by training little and often early on.

| Cricket | One of the world's oldest games, it is also one of the most old-fashioned. The idea of proper warm-up has only recently crept into the game (since the one-day professional game became popular), and photos of England captain Bob Willis doing stretching exercises still have a curiosity value. The best fielders of recent years have always been 'on their toes'—as you have to be in a sport where sudden movements can cause strains and sprains. |

Apart from the obvious dangers and discomforts threatened by the use of a hard ball, cricketers suffer shoulder, back and knee problems. **A/C joint** strain is a classic example of an injury that prevents overarm bowling or throwing, though side and underarm efforts are painfree. Hard throws from the boundary reflare the injury, so either field closer or be satisfied with *threatening* a hard throw—and then return underarm. Cortisone injections may be required.

With the **Subacromial bursa**, the overarm bowling action is painless but hard overarm throws hurt. Treat with cortisone injections and throw in side or underarm.

Bowlers' backs suffer. If a right-arm fast bowler finds that leaning backwards and to the left and touching the toes hurts, it could be **Bowler's back**. Lying on the back and raising the left leg may also produce pain in the back. The outswing action can induce this as the bowler attempts to gain more speed or dig the ball in. Look at the **Low back pain** section and use the self-manipulation techniques. Rest, bowl slow and gradually build up to swing bowling rhythm, but try rotating the left foot outwards by degrees so that the left side 'clears' on delivery without locking and manipulating the facet joint. As you build up speed again, avoid 'digging it in' until painfree.

Knee problems like **Quads expansion, Chondromalacia patellae** and **Lower patella pole** are common in close fielders but usually occur (for right-arm bowlers) in the left leg at delivery. **Lower patella pole** is more common with inswing bowlers, who are balanced on the left knee for a fraction longer on delivery. The answer could be to cut down on speed and concentrate on away swingers until painfree.

Slip fielders who spend hours bobbing up and down, putting stress on their quads, would benefit from strengthening exercises.

If cricketers at all levels thought more about stretching and specific fitness, they would have fewer aches and pains—and play better, too!

Cycling

The bicycle itself governs many of the aches and pains suffered by cyclists. Pains in the bottom can be caused by incorrect clothing or an uncomfortable or poorly positioned saddle (height? too far forward or back?). A numb penis or persistent erection due to pressure on certain nerves should be reported to a doctor if they persist. If boils occur, ensure that clothing is clean and that body hair has not grown back into the skin, causing infection. Hand pain often occurs in novices, but gloves and padded handlebars help. Lack of confidence in awkward conditions (cobbles, mud) leads to gripping too tightly—but beware numbness in the fourth and little fingers: the **Ulnar nerve** is being pinched. Numbness in the thumb, first and second fingers could be **Carpal tunnel syndrome**.

Weight must be evenly distributed over the hands, legs and bottom, but putting in a special effort leads to grimacing, which tenses the neck and upper back muscles. Try to smile, avoid grinding the teeth—relax!

Knees and ankles suffer from overuse in a sport that demands riders 'put miles in their legs'. This may sound like sacrilege, but if you hurt from **Quads pull, Quads extension, Chondromalacia patellae** or **Lower patella pole**—get off your bike. Use patter, skipping and swimming routines. Restart using low gears, build up slowly to high gears, and avoid climbing hills until high gears on the flat are painfree.

As riders lean forward in the racing position, acid can tip out of the stomach causing 'heartburn'. Stomach gas can press on the diaphragm, so take antacids (or oil of peppermint on a sugar lump) before races. If a bike frame is too small for you, or the handlebars too low, this can cause compression or 'springing' over the lower ribs. The correct comfortable riding position should be worked out with a coach. One tip on saddle height—sit upright and the heel of the leg (fully extended) should touch the pedal. As the ball of the foot is used to ride, the leg would then be 90 per cent (correctly) extended.

Darts

This has boomed in Britain in recent years thanks to TV coverage. Youngsters who want to emulate the professionals might suddenly spend three or four hours practising—the result is **Dart thrower's elbow**, which is **Olecranon bursa**. The other hazard is dartitis, where a player gets the equivalent of writer's cramp—and just cannot release the arrow! This can be as much psychological as physical!

Diving and Trampolining

Divers are usually carefully coached, graduating from exercise to exercise. There are relatively few 'impact' injuries from hitting the board and breaking the fingers on reverse or inward dives; even more rare are head injuries from spinning above the board and hitting it coming down. More frequent are strains and sprains of the hand, thumb, wrist and even shoulders in highboard diving, where divers hit the water repeatedly at 60 mph (100 kph). Back strain from piked one-and-a-half somersaults is common, due to the twist movement and arching of the back. Some incidence of **Osgood Schlatter's disease** has been noted amongst young divers on takeoff or 'springing' the board too frequently.

Trampolining certainly looks a 'fun' sport, but *must* be supervised at all times. Surprisingly, a large number of injuries are suffered in folding and unfolding the powerful, spring-loaded beds. This is not a job for children. Painful joint instability (wrist, shoulder, ankle and knee) is common, and many accidents among youngsters occur due to the *G* (gravity) forces exerted that make them black out for a moment, lose control and land awkwardly. In spite of high safety levels, there are still a worrying number of accidents in the sport, and medical experts in many countries recommend that trampolining should *not* be a school sport because of the inherent competi- tiveness that this encourages. Awkward neck injuries may cause tetraplegia (see Head warning, p 39).

Equestrian sports

Riders at all levels can be seen making basic mistakes. Whether the event is showjumping, dressage or the cross-country phase of a three-day event, a rider should use the same technique and balance to guide the horse. The rider should sit in the classic 'A' frame position with the shoulder over the hipbone and the hands should be kept steady—'a steady hand means a steady mouth'.

Hands that look as if they are ringing the bells of Westminster Cathedral make the horse suffer. Riders should be relaxed, because any stiffness through the shoulder and down in the elbow will cause aches and pains. The elbows are the 'shock absorbers' for the wrists, so must be relaxed. Another fault is to ride 'unevenly', with, say, one leg further forward than the other in the stirrups. Any technical faults can lead to strains, and if they unbalance the horse, result in falls.

Riders: (a) must lean in on their corners—the body must not go against the movement of the horse; (b) should avoid 'fixing' their hands—they should be flexible at the wrists; (c) must communicate through the aids one gives a horse to make movements.

In jumping, many riders are inclined to look down. This places the shoulder in front of the knees and toes and unbalances the horse. As knee strength is so important, training the quads muscles off the horse is invaluable.

Falls should be dealt with by first-aid principles— beware neck injuries (see Head warning, p 39).

Fencing

Fencers can often get away with a low level of fitness. However, the chances are they won't be very competent. Endurance, strength and flexibility are all required to get to the top. Equipment must be checked frequently (especially masks) because any defect can result in injury. However blunt a sword may look, the lunging force behind it is considerable and penetration can be fatal. Look for signs of rusting on your face mask (from breathing on it!) and always strap on gear properly. If you are an occasional fencer, lower the risk of injury by stretching properly. In competition, repeated bouts are tiring because fencing suits promote high fluid loss. High glucose fluids, special fluid energy drinks or plain water will maintain fluid balance and blood sugar levels and put off fatigue.

Football, American and Canadian

Football is an organized, supervised sport where techniques are usually carefully taught. There is a right and a wrong way to block, tackle, pass, etc. Learn the right way or risk an injury. The major problems of 20 years ago (neck, knee and ankle injuries) are now less acute as the advice of sports medicine experts has been heeded. Of course, every part of the body is liable to damage in the ultimate in contact sports.

Major improvements in helmet design to give more protection and support have reduced neck injuries. Players with neck problems should wear a rubber collar. 'Spearing' can cause horrific injuries and is rightly an ejection offence. As the use of hands and arms is now more freely allowed, players tackle in a more upright stance, using their heads less and avoiding the head-to-head clashes that used to cause spinal compression.

New rules about blocking below the waist have cut down knee and ankle injuries, as have better shoes and judicious use of taping. Players' fitness and flexibility are better, with training schedules more specific, to, say, strengthen the neck and upper body. On the other hand, overenthusiasm can produce overuse injuries from weight-training. Modern equipment is lighter and less restrictive, but players should never wear defective or ill-fitting gear.

Mid-back pain can be caused by pushing or blocking with a rounded back. Ensure **back strain position** (p 64) in all back-strengthening exercises. Teenagers are especially prone to overloading this area. As most blocking and tackling strains that cause **Back pain** do not pull muscles but rather damage a disc or facet joint, seek early medical advice and do not play without medical permission.

Training and playing on artificial turf may cause **Black toe/Turf toe**. Try padding along the sides of the big toe or tongue of the shoe to hold the width of the foot more firmly and so prevent it driving into the shoe toe on checking.

Some injuries have names like halfback hamstring, but this is not specific to the sport. As in rugby, baseball, etc., where players may stand idle for periods and then sprint suddenly, the hamstring is always likely to suffer if not kept stretched and warm.

Jersey finger is common to other sports too. A quick grab at a player as he rushes by can result in a painful tweak (even **Mallet finger**) to the top joint of the finger.

Golf

Aches and pains are common, as for most golfers the game is their only exercise. The modern trend of golf-carts exacerbates the problem by eliminating walking—the only exercise in the game and a way to keep limber between shots.

The twisting action of a drive or chip tends to produce aches in the trunk, hips and knees, whilst the elbows and shoulders suffer from poor technique. **High back pain** is made worse merely by rotation, so seek medical advice. Early manipulation may ease pain. **Shoulderblade rub** is often made worse or produced by a very tense, hunched-back address with the arms held straight and rigid. The weight is often over the toes and pick-up is 'pushed', with extended arms too far backwards, so that the weight drops onto the front foot. The answer is to sit back, relax the shoulders and arm and check your stance with a golf pro.

Arthritis of the hip will require a hand–arm swing, but if limited to the left hip open the stance and allow for a fade.

Shoulder pain requires rest and medical advice. However, putting should be painfree, so practise that. After all, 'you drive for show, and putt for dough!'. Build back, using the ladder plan principle, through chip shots, short irons and, when troublefree, mid and long irons and woods.

Two frequent elbow pains are **Golfer's elbow** and **Tennis elbow**. Golfer's elbow occurs in the right arm of the righthander, usually due to an open right-hand grip. At the address the weight is forward, and the takeaway continues to keep the weight on the front foot. This blocks the full takeaway, so the swing is continued by cocking the wrists early. Sometimes the right hand will release on the club at the top of the swing. This produces a slice which the golfer controls by locking his right elbow into his side at the top of the swing. Therefore, the only way to generate power is by pulling hard and early with the right hand. See your pro.

Tennis elbow in the right arm is usually caused by a closed right-hand grip with weight on the front foot. The takeaway is then made with exaggeratedly straight arms and by dipping the left shoulder, usually without proper rotation. See your pro. With tennis elbow in the left arm, weight is often forward at the address, the left wrist carried high and forward of the club. Pick-up is often initiated by wrist, rather than shoulder movement. Club-head speed is increased on release through the shot by straightening the left wrist. More trouble occurs if a big divot is taken on hard ground or the rough blocks the shot. Again, correct your technique.

Gymnastics

The demand for perfection causes overuse injuries as techniques are continuously repeated by youngsters. Despite the boom, not everyone is built for the sport, so medical advice should be heeded when it comes to **Swayback elbow** for example. There are obvious injuries from falls, and in men's gymnastics (which are 'all arms') the shoulders suffer. Large protective callouses are characteristic of the sport, too (see: Common ailments, p 32).

Gymnast's back can be divided into two main causes. When a youngster tries to achieve too much too soon, hyperextension of the back is concentrated on one spot. Correct by increasing shoulder mobility and train extension of the spine to be spread all down the lower spine in a smooth arch rather than an acute angle. Overworking the trail leg in backward and the lead leg in forward walkovers can cause back pain, too. Try alternating lead legs (difficult!) and lengthen the arc of the circle. Rest if necessary from walkovers.

The wrist takes a lot of stress, and a **Stress fracture of**

the radius tends to occur in the fulcral or pivotal wrist of twisting vaults. The Tsukahara may be most to blame. All training that hurts the wrist must be avoided, but the beam and bars should be alright in the earliest days of the injury. Maintain stretching, and after about four weeks, when weight can be taken on the wrist without pain, handstands can be tried. Using the ladder principles (see p 104), graduate to walkovers (**no** flick-flacks, somersaults), and when healed, via straight vaults, flick-flacks, somersaults, twisting vaults, to Tsukaharas. Avoid heavy-twisting vault sessions; preferably, alternate with other routines every other day. Check with a doctor on balancing progress and training.

The force of landing hard after a dismount (overrotating forwards, underrotating backwards) can cause **Quads pull, Quads expansion, Chondromalacia patellae, Lower patella pole** and **Osgood Schlatter's disease** problems. When too painful to land, do no vaults or dismounts. Work on the bars, the beam (without squat) and check on the mat that walkovers are troublefree. Do floor suppling and arm balance and build in to walkovers as the condition improves. Then using the ladder system build up via dismounts, rolling out of landing; for vaults, roll out of forward landing or into the vaulting pit. Only then 'spot' dismounts and landings. Try to avoid heavy floor and vault training on the same day—do floor and bar alternated daily with vault and beam.

Impingement injury to ankle can also be caused by overrotating forwards and underrotating backwards on landing. Roll out of landings until better; save 'spotted' landings for competition. Correct the technical fault.

Swayback elbow or hyperextension is caused when the elbow is straightened too far. There is acute pain in the joint. The injury is common in gymnastics where competitors spend as much time on their hands as their feet. While the normal elbow can go 5 or 10 degrees beyond 180, the swayback elbow goes back even further, straining the ligaments that hold the upper and lower armbones together. Rest completely, although muscle-stretching exercises may be continued for shoulders and legs. Olympic-style gymnasts with swayback elbows are strongly advised to consider switching to another type of sport such as rhythmic gymnastics or trampolining sooner rather than later. Repeated injuries destroy confidence, technical faults develop in an effort to get round the problem, and complex moves can be dangerous under these circumstances.

Handball   See under Basketball.

Hockey, Field	The use of artificial turf and the growth of indoor hockey has produced 'new' injuries in a game characterized by the need to run in a 'bent' position over the stick. This can result in **High knee hip**, which flares up after long and unaccustomed training sessions, especially if dribbling the ball. Artificial surfaces increase the driving style of running with the ball on the open stick. It is necessary to build up gradually to this style and vary training sessions to allow rest.

Footballer's groin occurs in hockey, especially on hard or artificial surfaces where defenders back off, twisting and turning from side to side. When fit, build up gradually through 'dummy and reverse stick pull', restart play in wing-half position and channel opponents one way (warn the fullback which way!).

Quads pull, **Quads expansion**, **Chondromalacia patellae** or **Lower patella pole** problems can be caused for the stick-stopper trapping the ball during excessive practice sessions for short corner drills. Have short, sharp sessions rather than long ones.

Jumper's ankle occurs in hockey in the left foot of players (especially left-wingers at speed) who stamp hard (particularly on artificial turf) before reverse stick check. Switch position until healed or use a shorter running stride.

Black toe/Turf toe is common on dry, artificial turf when a sudden stop drives the toe into the front of the shoe. In hockey, the turf should be watered for matches, but avoid competitive training regimes that involve fast stops on dry turf.

Veterans often suffer **Hamstring** injuries due to lack of suppleness as they 'run and bend' to collect a ball or to tackle, so they should maintain stretching and fitness. Blows on the hands are common. ICE bruises as soon as possible, but check for fractures. With the added pace when shooting the ball on hard and artificial surfaces, goalkeepers must wear correct protection—this is not 'soft' but sensible. |
Horse-riding	See Equestrian sports.
Jogging	See under Track and field athletics.
Judo	One of the most disciplined sports in the world, where players learn techniques under supervision, are only matched against players of similar ability and size, and learn to fall and throw properly from the start. The last thing a judo player wants to do is to injure an opponent. It requires great strength and endurance, speed and agility. Youngsters can suffer a 'pulled elbow', where the head of the radius 'pops out' of alignment. It can be 'clicked' back

into place by a qualified person. Because players often resist throws with the fist clenched, judo elbow is produced, with a pain on both sides of the joint, often described as a combination of **Tennis** and **Golf elbow**.

Apart from general twists and strains, there are disfigurements like **Cauliflower ears** and even permanently bent fingers where a player has repeatedly used a favourite technique that strains ligaments and results in joint displacement. In long tournaments where several rounds are contested, fluid balance is important; but at the other end of the scale, the club that has to meet in a back room must ensure that there are no dangerous projecting objects.

Kayaking	See under Canoeing.
Netball	See under Basketball.
Racquetball	See under Squash.

Rowing

Rowers must make sure that their equipment is properly set up to suit their needs. As fitness demands increase, so do injuries from dryland training. **Chondromalacia patellae** is one example where too much quads work causes pain. This can be helped by placing a backstop on the slide at a distance that ensures the knees straighten. The slide must hit the backstop with each stroke.

In the boat, **High back pain** is often a facet or joint pain but may be felt in the ribs or the chest ('feels like a fractured rib'—but isn't). The cause is overreaching on the stroke or sudden loss of boat balance when catching the water. Manipulate early. **Mid-back pain** can also be caused by overreaching producing a hunched middle-back position. Ensure back strain position through the stroke. Take any weight-training slowly, ensuring correct technique. The gripping and twisting action of rowing produces **Paddler's wrist** (see Canoeing, p 133) (tenosynovitis of the wrist/De Quervain's), where the long tendon and sheath of the thumb are inflamed in the wrist and forearm. Cross-frictional massage, ultrasound and an injection of cortisone may help, but surgery may be required to release constriction of the sheath. Beginners who try to do too much in one go may suffer this. It usually occurs in the feathering hand. Experienced rowers may flare the inside hand by an alteration in the oar handle size (too small, too large), or in rough weather, or even if the gate is too tight.

Rugby Union, League

In a game that involves catching and passing a ball, proper techniques must be learnt to minimize finger

injuries (**Mallet fingers**) as well as increase ability.
Tackling and taking a tackle properly are important
—again, both for efficiency as well as avoiding injury.
Players should not 'freeze' when tackled but learn to roll
and fall, like a parachutist, or else damage to the inside
and outside of the knee joint is likely.

Hamstring problems are common amongst the backs,
who have to stand around doing nothing, waiting for the
ball. However, proper stretching can lower the risk,
especially amongst the explosive, shortstepping sprinters
like halfbacks, who tend to have shorter hamstrings. Backs
should never stand still but always keep loose, moving,
ready.

Forwards need to have powerful necks and backs.
Special training is especially necessary at schoolboy level,
where a worrying number of paralysis injuries have been
incurred in recent years. This can be due to
mismatching—boys of similar age rather than size.
Incorrect scrummaging causes aches and pains, too. A
useful tip is to do plenty of 'swallows' as well as 'sit-ups'.

In a game of physical contact, **Concussion** is not
uncommon; bruising of the brain has occurred, so avoid
playing (but keep fit) for at least three weeks. When **Neck
pain** occurs amongst forwards, it could be lack of specific
strength and discs could have been moved. The so-called
'tactic' of dropping the scrum is made deliberately illegal;
it is lethal and murderous and could paralyse a player for
life.

Back pain is not caused by 'pulling a muscle' during a
ruck or maul, but by damage to a disc or facet joint. Seek
medical advice and do not play until advised. Ensure back
strain position (p 64) in the scrum.

Shoulders take the brunt of falls, often producing the
A/C joint injury. Use a sling early on and avoid
weight-training of the arms until cured. Seek medical
help, because in rare cases forwards may need surgery.

Groin strains can be dealt with using the ladder
principle: build up the sidestep gradually through the
knee run (p 110), but beware violent sidesteps that may
produce **Footballer's groin**. Build into punting and
kicking, looking for easy rhythm and accuracy until
painfree. Then add length.

With the increased emphasis on training which is often
built more on myth and tradition than science, using
weights that are too heavy for too long will produce
injuries. **Quads strain**, **Quads expansion**,
Chondromalacia patellae and **Lower patella pole** are
typical examples in the knee. Forwards may benefit from
changing from open to blind side, especially the props,
taking the load off the painful leg. Goal kickers may flare
the injury after a long session using a heavy ball. A tackle

blocking the kicking leg whilst punting or even a tackle preventing completion of the knee straightening (while running) can cause **Quads pull**. If **Torn cartilage ligaments** are the problem, avoid using the bad knee when getting up during training sessions. Props can benefit from changing from loose to tight head (or vice versa) if the front knee is the problem. Ugly **Cauliflower ears** can be prevented by using a sweatband.

Running

See under Track and field athletics.

Sailing

'Water, water everywhere nor any drop to drink' was the sailor's nightmare—and still can be in competitions that start early and can finish late. Take drinks, using plastic bottles with plastic straws, so that you can have something while racing. The presence of water always means a risk of hypothermia, so wear the right gear.

The leaning, bending and pulling required gives the back and stomach muscles a fair workout, but in larger boats larger loads can cause strains and correct techniques must be used to avoid rope damage to hands.

'Silly accidents' can be avoided by thinking—so don't put your hands over the side of the gunwale, they could be crushed by another boat making contact. Know the distance between the bottom of the boom and the top of the deck or centreboard case. Don't stand near coils of heavy-duty rope, and keep your hands and fingers well away from winches and pulleys.

Knee ligaments can suffer when the dinghy helmsman is forced to sit in an awkward position. Try other positions—or even change the type of boat if the trouble persists.

Shooting

Apart from accidents with weapons, there are few injuries in the sport. Shoulders and faces can be bruised and even cut due to 'kick', which is made worse by a badly fitting gun. Avoid by: (a) getting a gun of the correct size and shape (i.e. correct mounting and good stock fitting) and (b) holding the gun more firmly. The thumb should always be curled around the stock, *not* left behind the top lever, which can come back and damage the thumb. When the gun is held thus, there should be three fingers' space between thumb and nose.

Coming back to safety, a broken gun should be assembled by moving the stock to the barrel with the barrel pointing at the ground, so any accidental discharge goes into the ground. Relatively few accidents result from discharge into the foot, but if the barrel is raised to the stock more accidents occur as the discharge could go anywhere.

Housemaid's knee may occur in the kneeling position

of three-position rifle shooting. A padded plastic or rubber knee pad helps. No-one should shoot without earmuffs—to do so risks acoustic trauma, damage to hearing. At competitive level there is a vogue for drugs called beta-blockers to slow the pulse and control tremor, but the advantage is doubtful. Many shooters require the drugs for medical reasons (heart trouble, high blood pressure). Alcohol in moderation helps some.

Skating, Ice	Speed skating, because of its 'forward lean', may produce **High knee hip pain**. Training should be built up gradually, and during the off-season hip strength should be maintained with squat thrusts, Burpees and running with the body leaning forward. Use a short hockey stick and run with it.

In artistic or figure skating, the top performers are injured because of the huge jumps and spins attempted but not always completed. At lower levels, when **Quads pull**, **Quads expansion**, **Chondromalacia patellae**, **Lower patella pole** and **Osgood Schlatter's disease** pains occur, avoid jumps until better. Work on tracing figures and straight-line step sequence. When improving, try to alternate days for work on jumps. Although the ice/skate contact is unyielding, knee injuries from jumping and landing are not common until bigger jumps are attempted. **Stress fractures** may occur through repeating the same jump too often in one session. The check and pick of the foot with rotation causes strain through the legbones, especially from triple Lutzes. Plan the week so that jump sessions are not too long in any one day, and if possible alternate days of jumps and no jumps. **Tailbone pain (coccygitis)** is very painful and can be caused by repeated falling: it is more frequent among women. Ice hockey injuries are primarily from violent physical contact. Skater's heel is often the result of wearing boots that are tight in the heel, so make sure they fit properly if you intend to skate a lot.

Skiing	Most skiers are holidaymakers who do little or no physical preparation. Thanks to modern boot and binding design as well as better instruction, injuries are less frequent than they used to be. However, good stretching and preparation can minimize accidents further. Get the best ski bindings; don't have them too tight and ensure that they are properly mounted, set and oiled. Pain, numbness or pins and needles that persist over the top of the foot and the big toe can be caused by pressure of the boots on a nerve, either in the leg at the top front of the ankle or over the forefoot. Improve the padding, loosen off or get a larger pair of boots.

Medial ligament strain and **Torn cartilage**

ligaments usually occur in the less good skier, who cannot parallel properly and so turns by checking with the edge of the downhill ski and locking the knees into the hill with bodyweight back. Try pushing the tip of the outside ski down over moguls (bumps) to get the weight forward and roll out the weight through the knees and ankles. Holding the back strain position (p 64) may help weight adjustment. Good skiers probably have their bindings too tight if they have knee problems.

Quads pull, **Quads expansion**, **Chondromalacia patellae**, **Lower patella pole** and **Osgood Schlatter's disease** are flared by fast runs in the 'egg' position, so keep off runs where leg work will be hard. Relax on easier runs in the upright position.

In cross-country skiing, **Anterior compartment pain** is an overuse injury caused when the toes and forefoot are lifted towards the shinbone on the prolonged forward glide, especially on hard uphill sessions. Build up strength with toe-hold sit-ups. **Tennis elbow** is an overuse injury caused by the rhythmic plant of the skipole and twisting to free it for the next stride. Skier's thumb occurs when the ligaments at the base of the thumb are torn because the skipole is held too tightly.

Holidaymakers who would worry about going to the altitude of Mexico City think nothing of exerting themselves in the mountains. But dehydration and altitude sickness (nausea, dizzy spells, headaches, tiredness) are common. Take liquid—not alcohol—and allow time to adjust. As snow reflects 85 per cent of the sun's burning rays, use sunglasses and a sunscreen recommended by your doctor. Zinc oxide blocks all rays. On cross-country runs, remember to take an outward course that leaves you enough energy to get back comfortably! Replace liquids frequently. Mittens are warmer than gloves, and if the extremities (nose, ears, toes, fingers) go numb and red, keep moving so that the circulation has a chance to help. The head loses a lot of heat—wear a woolly hat.

Skindiving	See under Swimming.
Soccer	Cuts, bruises and broken bones are common enough, but most injuries are in the lower limbs. **Footballer's groin** is a relatively new complaint, thought to be brought on by the one-sided load of kicking. In defenders, it is flared by backing off and twisting from side to side. Too many players return to the game too soon. Beware! When fit for sprints, use the Achilles top ladder, and at step 7 start a simultaneous kicking ladder—juggle ball; stroke ball 10 m/yd; chip; drive and volley; inside of foot drive; hooked kick; tackle gently; lower-level game, channelling opponents one way only; match fit.

Adductor strains are often caused by overstretching sideways or a blocked sidefoot tackle. Use the kicking ladder (above) to build back. **Quads pull** can be the result of someone blocking your leg as you straight drive or volley the ball. However, **Quads expansion, Chondromalacia patellae, Lower patella pole** and **Osgood Schlatter's disease** are usually caused in training rather than match play, when a long session plus hard kicking, especially with a heavy ball, flares the injury. Alter the training and reduce quads strength training.

The twisting strains of ball control are particularly severe on the knee and **Torn cartilage ligaments** can result. Avoid close dribbling in training, especially when carrying the ball with the injured leg. Checking the ball with the outside of the foot can cause trouble. Defenders—channel attackers so that you turn on your good side (or even switch sides of the field to make this easier) and tell covering teammates which way you will channel. In training, do not do bunny hops—and avoid using the bad leg when getting up from the ground.

Front of ankle joint strain occurs after repeated kicking of a heavy ball or after a drive is blocked. Use stirrup strapping (p 89) on both sides of the ankle to try to prevent the foot being forced down when driving the ball. Build up through chip and side foot to drive and volley in practice.

Jumper's ankle can occur, too, if a blocked drive kick forces the heelbone onto the back of the shin. It is probably safe to play, but the injury will not settle until treated medically. **Footballer's ankle** occurs as players use their feet to put spin on the ball, chip it, pass it with quick flicks, or get kicked.

Softball

See under Baseball.

Squash/Racquetball

These are classic games for 'getting fit'. So convenient for time, easy to take up—but dangerous to play with a friend when beginning. Play within the boundaries of your own fitness, because it is easy to overdo it. It is not 'soft' to wear proper eye protection, as the ball fits the eye socket neatly—and that's dangerous. The hard floors can produce blisters and **Black nail**, and in hot climates fluid intake is important. Shoulder injuries are common. Pain in the **A/C joint** is usually no trouble unless you play a lot of overheads, so avoid smashes and take off the back wall—unless it's a vital match! Using a flying elbow instead of rotating properly may cause trouble on the forehand, but in severe cases the backhand may hurt. Seek medical advice. If you suffer from **Painful arc** (caused by squash) you should check with a coach, as your technique would need correcting. The **Subacromial bursa** usually only flares in smashing hard, or, occasionally, with high, tense take-away of elbow and shoulder on the forehand. Relax shoulder tension and go for rhythm and less power.

Squash player's finger is caused by using a closed grip with the index finger extended too far down the shaft and holding too tightly, causing pain in the bulky muscle on the back of the hand between thumb and index finger. Use the third, fourth and fifth fingers to grip. **Quads pull**, **Quads expansion**, **Chondromalacia patellae** and **Lower patella pole**, **Jumper's knee** and **Osgood Schlatter's disease** may all cause trouble over the knee on the racquet-hand side. **Pronator terres syndrome** is caused by faulty technique, where the forehand is played with the racquet-hand below the wrist. Injury occurs trying to angle the shot straight to the front wall on forehand retrieve instead of hitting the boast. Correct the fault.

Outer strap tendon pains may be induced by rolling over the outer side of the foot when playing backhand (especially in the sport of rackets when trying to impart more spin). Alter your technique and use a lateral wedge, ankle support or stirrup strapping.

Tennis elbow/squash elbow is caused by either a lack of forearm strength and/or faulty technique. On the forehand, using a closed grip, the index finger is forced too far along the handle and there is a tendency to drop the racquet head and play an arm shot with the elbow flying and lack of rotation. In a faulty backhand, the racquet head drops and a high elbow leads the racquet into a shot. Correct your technique and check that your grip is not held tightly by thumb and forefinger. Try a thicker handle and grip with the third, fourth and fifth fingers. Use the squash ladder to get back to fitness.

Surfing	See under Swimming.
Swimming/Skindiving/ Surfing/Waterpolo	Swimming is regarded as the ideal form of exercise because it is so injury-free. However, everyone should know that it is dangerous to swim soon after a meal; stomach cramp is possible. Chlorine in pools, if too strong, can bleach hair and sting the eyes, while verruca warts can be caught from the damp floors of public poolsides. If you have them, wear rubber swimsocks to be fair to others. Physical problems only really emerge when swimmers become competitive, putting in 50,000 m (approx. 50,000 yd) a week combined with heavy dry land training—the result is overuse injuries like swimmer's shoulder (**Painful arc, Shoulder impingement, Subacromial bursa**). **Crawler's compression** is caused by applying

shoulder power before completion of arm recovery. This 'striking too soon' may also cause swimmer's shoulder.

In the breaststroke there can be knee ligament problems which can be corrected by reducing the width of the leg kick to the width of the shoulders and increasing the backward kick. Free style and butterfly can produce lower back, patella and lower femur problems which are corrected by improving the quality of the stroke as well as by reducing distance in training. For extreme butterfly problems change the stroke and practise backstroke for a while.

Skin or scuba diving has its inherent safety problems which must never be treated lightly. The 'bends' are a decompression sickness where gas forms in the bloodstream; 'rapture of the depths' is nitrogen narcosis; burst lungs are the result of an air embolism. Are we stating the obvious by pointing out that they can be fatal? There are enough unnecessary accidents to show that nothing is obvious. Stick to the safety drill *all the time*.

Surfing is dangerous thanks to a combination of fast-moving water and boards that can knock a swimmer senseless. However, there are two or three afflictions peculiar to the sport. Wax rash can be helped by wearing a T-shirt, since the rash is caused by lying on the board. The T-shirt also prevents sunburn. Surfer's foot is a painful growth at the head of the first metatarsal bone produced because the body's weight is over the instep of one foot when propelling the board out to sea. Wetsuit rub is cured by applying petroleum jelly to the sore part and checking that the suit fits properly.

Waterpolo is one of the roughest sports around, but apart from the results of physical contact, the shoulders can suffer stiffness due to overuse. Rest is the only cure, though competitive players prefer to put up with the pain rather than stop their sport. Cold water can cause problems in the last quarter.

Table Tennis	One of the most injury-free sports, but because it is so popular and can be played anywhere tables are often on hard floors. Make sure footwear is well padded to avoid blisters and bruising.
Tennis	One of sport's most famous ailments is **Tennis elbow**, which can be caused by lack of forearm strength as well as by technical faults. Sometimes an awkward bounce can flare the injury, too. If you play your forehand with a closed grip and hit the ball with an open stance, you will tend to have an 'arm only' swing without shoulder rotation. The racquet head is too low and the elbow is put under stress. Correct your technique. It is interesting to note that players using the

two-handed backhand suffer from little or no tennis elbow. However, how often do you see a sloppy backhand punch, with the ball 'pushed' with the elbow. The elbow should be tucked in, pointing towards the ground, not the net. When the racquet head is below wrist-level and the high wrist leads into the shot, the power is generated by the wrist, so the elbow suffers. Correct your technique. Also, try a thicker racquet grip with a lighter-weight head and less taut stringing. Use the ladder plan (p 122) to regain fitness. Abdominal strains can be troublesome. Don't 'snatch' at topspin service and cut down pace.

Radiohumeral joint/Triceps strain can be the result of tension during a match, which often makes you grip your racquet more tightly with thumb and index finger. This prevents the wrist from releasing, especially in topspin service, causing a snapping effect at the elbow which may also flare the triceps. Relax this thumb/index finger pressure, cut down the speed and jerk of your service, ensure the ball is being thrown in front and hit through the shot. See a coach.

Pronator terres syndrome is usually caused when retrieving a forehand shot that is nearly past you, so the racquet head is dropped below the wrist. Correct the technical fault. With all the running involved (and good footwork is essential), **Arthritis** or **Rigid toe** injury in the big toe may occur. When the service action levers across the big toe of the back foot, this can flare the big toe joint. Try a jump serve to avoid this. The repetitive serve action will always reflare a damaged **A/C joint**, which will require rest and treatment. However, bad technique may strain the shoulder muscles, and power generated at the shoulder may produce **Subdeltoid bursa, Shoulder impingement** or **Subacromial bursitis**. Tennis is a game for all ages, but shoulder problems due to alteration in circulation occur more frequently in the older person. Ground strokes can usually be improved whilst the shoulder is being treated, and also remember that leg and knee injuries should not prevent you from practising strokes against a tennis-training machine.

Track and Field Athletics

There is something for everyone in a sport where more time is spent training than competing. Most of the injuries occur in the legs and are covered earlier in the book but some ailments are peculiar to different events. Imitating a champion's training method may not be right for your shape and size. Quantity is no substitute for quality in running events, so more miles do not necessarily mean better results. Artificial tracks are quite hard (as are roads), so train on grass when it comes to quantity. Keep your quality for the track. Track and field nuts tend to be swayed by fads—diets, vitamins, even equipment.

There is no evidence that any of these improve performance.

Groin strain, Adductor muscle strain and Adductor pull-off:
Sprints: 1 Delay block starts until healed, then cruise out starts over the first week to build up adductor strength. 2 Bend running should be built up from the outside lane. After 6 runs without pain, move in a lane. Repeat.
Hurdles: Beware the complication of **Footballer's groin**, especially with high hurdles.
Discus: Jerky rotations can cause these problems. Concentrate on footwork.

Quads pulls, Quads expansion, Chondromalacia patellae, Lower patella pole and Osgood Schlatter's disease:
Sprints: Avoid weight-training and sprint starts for quads until healed. Use rolling starts.
Long, triple jump: Rest from jumping; work on speed. Beware of bounding and step-ups. Use the quads ladder.

Jumper's knee:
Repeated minor damage to the kneecap tendon produces thickening of the tendon lining. This may require surgery. It is important that quads and knee ladders are followed carefully, not rushed, or the injury will recur.

Cartilage ligament strain:
Pole vault: If the high knee approach is overemphasized, the lower leg may flail (or windmill) on the carry side to counterbalance upper body rotation. Check with a coach.

Medial ligament strain:
Sprints: Use a rolling start until painfree; use outer lanes for bend running.

Javelin thrower's elbow:
An overuse injury thought to be caused by round-arm technique and dangerous when occurring in growing youngsters. Seek medical advice, as a piece of bone may pull off. Takes 4–6 weeks to heal.

Hamstring pull:
Sprinters should watch their change of cadence as they go from the starting body angle to the more upright, flowing angle. Pull-off fractures are fairly common amongst teenagers.

Triple jumper's heel:
Heel cups help, but avoid jumping if possible. Work on speed; use standing jumps.

Shot putter's finger:
A sprain of the first three fingers from squeezing the shot to give a final acceleration to the putt. It is diagnosed by holding the hand vertical, then when straight fingers are lowered to 90° angle against pressure of the other hand, pain is confirmed on the inside of the fingers. Rest from throwing, tape (check for legality in competition) and use

ultrasound and cortisone injections. Omit finger
acceleration in training throws; save for competition.

Fosbury flop ankle:

Pain occurs on the outer side of the ankle in high jumpers
who use the flop style because they probably over-evert
the foot at plant for take-off. As the foot checks for rotation,
the momentum drives the central bone against the central hinge.
Using self-diagnosis, the foot hurts when the heel is forced
sideways and outwards, but does *not* hurt on forcing the
heel inwards or when pulling the toes downwards and
inwards. Rest will help, along with correction of the
technical fault. Cortisone injections, even surgery, may be
needed. Subsequent training should concentrate on heels,
quads, stretching. Maintain straight-line bounding and
depth jumping. Build into Fosbury rotation, straighten foot
plant.

Stress fractures:

Sprinters are particularly prone to these injuries,
especially when working on the Don Quarrie-like style of
accelerating the foot into the ground after a high knee lift.
Try the same movement without driving the foot onto the
ground. Long-distance runners—aim for heart/lung
fitness, running skill and endurance of the relevant bones
and muscles. Do not run distances that break your bones!
Rest them by interspersing a heart/lung session on your
pedal bike—your fitness will be the same and your body
won't fall apart! Try a varied weekly routine:

Monday—long, steady bike session (1 hr)
Tuesday—short run
Wednesday—long run
Thursday—bike session
Friday—rest
Saturday, Sunday—races

Joggers should ease into their sport. Running, however
slowly, along a beach with its hot, soft sand does the
Achilles tendon no good at all for a first-time workout.
Avoid running hard downhill. This is a great temptation
but jars the spine, knee, etc. Learn to run properly—it
really is more than putting one foot in front of the other. Get
the heel contact right, knee slightly bent, with an easy low
arm action to help the legs along. And to avoid running too
fast, too soon, try chatting, talking to yourself or a partner. If
you can't, you are going too fast.

Trampolining	See under Diving and trampolining.
Volleyball	See under Basketball.
Waterpolo	See under Swimming.

Waterskiing

Travelling at speed with the possibility of crashing will always mean that injuries are not far away. Water is much harder than you think when you hit it at speed, as is the shore if you dismount too late! Dismount parallel to the shore. Once you get to competition level, there are knee ligament problems. At lower levels, a good level of fitness is required to avoid knee and shoulder strains. Early overuse strains such as **Tennis elbow** (from holding the tow handle horizontally) may be eased by turning the handle vertical, loading the biceps muscles instead of the elbow.

Tow boats should always be manned by two. Skiers should wear life-jackets for safety as well as visibility. Starting and dismounting should take place away from swimmers as they can be injured by tow rope whiplash.

Beginners must ensure that wetsuits protect the groin area, otherwise a high-pressure enema (amusing to talk about but excruciatingly painful) can occur when water is forced up the front or back passage.

**Weightlifting/
Weight-training**

One fitness expert, Gordon Richards, considers weightlifting 'the most worrying sport' that he encounters, due to the availability of the equipment without qualified supervision. This, coupled with the competitive nature of man, so that two friends try to outlift one another, can cause unseen injuries, especially amongst youngsters.

Quads pull, **Quads expansion**, **Chondromalacia patellae**, **Lower patella pole** and **Osgood Schlatter's disease** are all likely when the quads muscles are overloaded. Build up weights gradually, and if the knees ache decrease weight and concentrate on lifting technique. Build up upper body strength. Knee supports may act like an outer skeleton, spreading the load from these pressure points. Remember that repeat training of squats and splits whilst sore will *not* allow these injuries to heal.

A dislocated elbow can occur if a weight is lifted with too much backward component instead of vertical acceleration. Trying to hold this weight above the head, especially in the snatch, may cause dislocation. Check the pulse. Use a sling. Get medical help.

Weight-trainers would do better with counterbalanced as opposed to free weights, so that they can sit down with the back supported (as in power gyms). It is worth remembering that weights give you strength (muscle power), not stamina or fitness.

Dehydration can be a problem as weightlifters try to get into the lowest weight category.

Wrestling

One of those sports which are well supervised and well coached, so there is a relatively low incidence of injury.

Basic throwing and falling techniques are essential.

Joints (shoulders, knees, ankles) suffer from the wrenches of both competition and training. Hands and wrists are hurt from bad falls, while **Cauliflower** or **Wrestler's ear** is a regular problem, though high school and college grapplers must wear protective headgear.

Dehydration can be a problem as wrestlers try to get into the lowest weight category to maximize their strength. The problem of combining weight control (diet) with top-level fitness (per cent of body fat) is different for each individual.

The testicles are always vulnerable, but the only answer is to train with the Samurai!

6

A–Z OF
MEDICAL TERMS

Sports doctors—all doctors—often use long and technical words for quite simple injuries. This can be worrying. There is no need to panic—just look up that word here. (See also: A–Z of treatments, chapter 2.)

Abdominal

Stomach muscle.

A/C joint/acromio clavicular joint

Joint between collarbone and shoulderblade; forms 'step' in shoulder if displaced.

Acromion

Bony point on top of shoulder; tip of shoulderblade.

Aerobics

Continuous exercise at ¾ speed and below; raises pulse rate to improve heart and lung function and muscles for greater stamina.

Anaemia

Insufficient red cells in blood; small measured variations do not alter athletic performance. May have number of causes but check with doctor, especially if periods heavy.

Anaerobic

Muscle exercise without oxygen; only lasts short time, with high pulse rate, e.g. explosive events like sprinting, weightlifting.

Anterior

Front.

Arthritis

Greek for 'inflammation of the joint'. Surface of joint wears away, resulting in pain. Switch sports to avoid stress and strain on joint.

Arthrogram

X-ray technique for joints using air and/or dye injected into affected joint, e.g. to show up torn cartilage.

Arthroscope

Modern technique using fibre-optics to probe complex joints like knee to track down injury and even operate without large incisions. Sort of 'telescope' that can look inside joint. Arthroscopy is name of operation.

Asthma

Constriction of tubes to lungs so breathing becomes difficult (see Some sensible tips, p 16).

Biceps

Bulging muscle on front of upper arm, the 'Popeye' muscle, used to bend elbow.

Biceps femoris

One of hamstring muscles.

Bursa

Sac of fluid that cushions or 'greases' movement of skin, muscles, tendons or ligaments across hard area and so stops them fraying (like string rubbing over brick). When inflamed, known as bursitis.

Calcaneus

Heelbone.

Capsule

Lining linking bone to bone; contains lubricating fluid for joint. See Ligament.

Cardiovascular

To do with heart and circulation. In sporting terms, implies ability to move oxygen from lungs to muscles and to get rid of carbon dioxide, body's exhaust fumes.

Cartilage

Smooth, slippery substance preventing two ends of bones rubbing, and thus grating, against each other. 'Torn cartilage': The knee has extra shock absorbers between the cartilage covered bones. Also made of cartilage, these are known as the cartilage or meniscus. They are so effective that complete removal leads to arthritis, so surgeons repairing a tear try to leave in as much as possible.

Chondromalacia

Roughening of slippery cartilage surface. Best known is chondromalacia patellae, or roughening of underside of kneecap.

Clavicle

Collarbone.

Congenital

From birth.

Contrast baths

Using heat followed by cold to increase blood flow.

Contusion

Bruise.

Costal

To do with ribs.

Crepitus

Grating feeling over damaged joint or tendon.

Cross-frictional massage

Technique of rubbing using small movements but firm pressure across line of muscle or tendon growth. Thought to break down scar tissue and realign fibres.

Deep friction massage

Uses firm pressure to get at deeper tissues.

Deltoids Muscles at top of arm, just below shoulder, which lift from about 20° at the side to 160°.

Diapulse Electrical instrument thought to help heal damaged cell wall.

Dorsiflex Bending foot and ankle upwards.

EMG Electromyogram Test to check how well nerve is working.

Extension Straightening joint.

Fast twitch fibre See White fibre.

Femur Thighbone, big bone in upper leg.

Fibula Smaller bone on outside of lower leg. Lower end forms outer anklebone.

Flexion Opposite of extension, i.e. bending joint.

Fracture Broken bone.

Gait Running or walking style.

Gastrocnemius Part of calf muscle (with Soleus).

Haematoma Packet of congealed blood, bigger and more serious than bruise, often raising lump as blood vessels are broken and bleed.

Hamstring Muscle at back of thigh that bends knee. Often injured through lack of proper pre-exercise stretching.

Humerus Bone of upper arm.

Impingement Banging together of two surfaces not normally in contact. Implies movements greater than normal range, e.g. acrobats arching backwards.

Inflammation Damage from overuse, wear and tear, disease—not from outside source.

Interferential Electrical machine to heat muscles and joints.

Isokinetic exercises Isokinetic means 'same energy'. Muscles vary in power in different positions, following principle of leverage. Sprinters start in crouch because more power is released from that position. Isokinetic machines are complex, costly and debatably efficient in training.

Isometric exercises Isometric means 'same length'. Two equal forces working against each other produce no movement. Used to test muscle and ligament pain, also to build strength. That strength is 'angle specific', i.e. only in position of exercise, not all positions. Exercises useful in early rehabilitation: press injured part against furniture or other arm or leg up to moment of pain, hold that level without retearing muscle. Helps strengthen scar in areas of greatest forces.

Isotonic exercises Isotonic means 'same tone'. For strength-building as in weightlifting or with now-popular 'variable resistance' machines in gymnasiums and health clubs. Idea is to shorten and lengthen muscles with same weight.

Laceration Cut.

Lactic acid Waste product of muscle energy. As this builds up, muscles cease to work. Sprint exercises build lactic acid faster, hence sudden 'loss of leg strength' at end of 400 m (440 yd).

Lateral Outer side of body.

Ligament Area strengthening joints, linking bone to bone, e.g. forearm to upper arm.

Medial Inner side of body.

Metacarpals Five bones of hand, just before fingers.

Metatarsals Five bones of foot, just before toes.

Microwave Not oven, but electrical equipment to heat deep tissues.

Osteochondritis diseases See under Knee, p 76.

Patella Kneecap.

Pectorals Chest muscles, beneath breast leading up to shoulder.

Plantarflex Bending foot and ankle downwards.

Quads/Quadriceps Muscles of thigh; these straighten knee.

Radius Forearm bone on thumb side.

Red fibre Part of muscle that maintains slower, weaker and longer-lasting work. Also known as Slow twitch fibre.

Referred pain Pain felt in undamaged area of body away from actual injury.

Scan	Injection of radioactive fluid (equal in radioactivity to about one X-ray) which may then be displayed on counting machine.
Scapula	Shoulderblade.
Sesamoid bone	Lies within and adds strength to tendons as they cover bony point; best known is kneecap.
Shortwave diathermy	Deep heat treatment on joints. (Also Interferential and Microwave.)
Slow twitch fibre	See Red fibre.
Soleus	Calf muscle.
Sprain	Damage to ligament or lining of joint.
Sternum	Breastbone.
Strain	Damage to muscle or tendon.
Stress fracture	Break in bone caused by continual repetition of movement.
Synovial fluid	Lubricating fluid for joints and tendons, produced in synovium, or inner lining of joint. Synovitis is damage to synovium.
Talus	Footbone that hinges in between two anklebones.
Tendon	Joins muscle to bone; unable to contract and relax; may be very long, as on back of hand. Tendinitis is damage to tendon.
Tenosynovitis	Inflammation of both tendon and sheath surrounding it.
Tibia	Larger of two bones in lower leg/shinbone.
Trauma	Damage caused by blow or outside source.
Triceps	Muscles in upper arm that extend elbow.
Ulna	One of two bones in forearm; forms point of elbow and lies on outer (little finger) side.
White fibre	Part of muscle that produces fast, strong but not long-lasting work; builds muscle bulk; does not need oxygen and fatigues fast. Also known as Fast twitch fibre.
Zyphisternum	Stomach end of breastbone; made of cartilage.